California Five-In-One Cook Book

Early California

•INDIAN •MEXICAN •MISSION •GOLD RUSH

California Fruits

•CITRUS •DATES •FIGS •NUTS •RAISINS •AVOCADOS •etc.

California Products

•HONEY •RICE •BEANS •BEEF •LAMB •TURKEY •VEGETABLES •etc.

Sea Foods

Wine Cooking

A COLLECTION OF MORE THAN 400 CALIFORNIA RECIPES

Compiled by
Al Fischer and Mildred Fischer

ARTWORK . . . by jerry a. hard & associates

Printed in the United States of America

Library of Congress Cataloging in Publication Data

Fischer, Al, 1923-
California five-in-one cook book.

Includes index.
1. Cookery, American--California. I. Fischer, Mildred, 1924- joint author. II. Title.
TX715.F5326 641.5'9794 76-10451
ISBN 0-914846-02-7

Golden West Publishers
4113 N. Longview Ave.
Phoenix, AZ. 85014, USA

Contents

EARLY CALIFORNIA

CALIFORNIA FRUITS

CALIFORNIA PRODUCTS

SEA FOODS

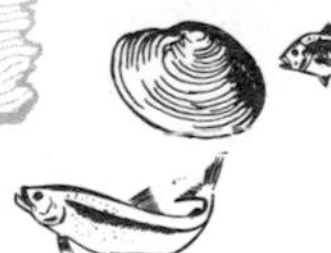

WINE COOKING

Early California

Indians of California, before the coming of the Spaniard, subsisted on whatever nuts, wild grains, seeds, berries, fruits, greens, roots and bulbs they could gather, and the wild game, birds, fish, shellfish and insects they could capture.

We call theirs the "acorn culture" because of their dependence on acorns from native oaks as a staple food. In order to make acorns palatable, it was necessary to leach the nuts of their tannic acid. This was done by running water through ground acorn meal. Leached meal was then made into a kind of mush or gruel and eaten with the hands. Often grains and other foodstuffs were included in the mush, or meat was added to make a stew. Rabbits, deer, quail and pheasants were abundant in the California wilds, clams and abalone were theirs for the taking along the coast, and, of course, fish were everywhere along streams and in the ocean.

Spanish settlers brought other products from distant parts of the New World and some from the Old World--corn, wheat, squash, beans, chick peas (garbanzos), numerous varieties of chili peppers, tomatoes, fruits, vegetables, grapes, olives, figs, oranges, chocolate, cattle, sheep, goats and hogs.

Life in the Spanish Missions depended on planting and harvesting. With corn came nixtamal, masa and tortillas. Two kinds of tortillas, corn and flour, were used as the staple "bread" or edible wrapper for many foods. Inside the missions, food consisted mainly of grain, fruits and vegetables. In the towns and on the rancheros, beef was added to the fare.

Today, descendants of Spanish and Mexican settlers prepare foods similar to those of their ancestors, including such ever-popular dishes as enchiladas, tacos, tostadas, burritos, tamales and other items wrapped in (or placed on) tortillas. In addition, Californians include chili con carne, albondigas, estofado, frijoles refritos on their menu--plus the sweet-tooth satisfying sopaipillas and Mexican chocolate.

The great whirlwind drive westward to California during the Gold Rush served to emphasize the importance of sourdough biscuits and beans, staple foods of early miners.

Immigrants who built California into the cosmopolitan center it has become brought with them from their homelands their favorite dishes--Cioppino, Portuguese Beans, Russian Tea--nourishing nostalgia.

ACORN STEW

2 lbs. lean BEEF CHUNKS
1 teaspoon SALT
1 cup ground, leached ACORN MEAL

Add water to cover beef chunks. Cook til tender (meat must be covered with water during cooking). Add salt while cooking. When meat is tender, separate from stock. Chop meat into small pieces and place in large serving bowl. Make paste of acorn meal and cold water; add to meat and mix thoroughly. Meat mixture will turn yellow from acorn meal. Pour stock over mixture, stir thoroughly, and heat before serving.

ROASTED PINON NUTS

Spread a pound of raw, shelled nuts in an ungreased shallow pan. Roast at 300 F about an hour, stirring frequently.

PINON NUT CAKES

2 cups PINON NUTS
¾ cup WATER
¼ to ½ teaspoon SALT
2 tablespoons OIL

Chop nuts coarsely and roll with rolling pin. Mix the meal with water and salt til batter is stiff. Let batter rest for an hour before frying. Pour oil into skillet and heat to sizzling. Drop batter from tablespoon into heated oil and form into six pancakes, shaping with greased pancake turner. Lower heat and flip cakes to brown evenly on both sides.

JUNIPER TEA

20 young JUNIPER SPRIGS
2 quarts cold WATER

Wash juniper sprigs and place in large pot. Add water and bring to a boil. Cover, reduce heat, and simmer for 15 minutes. Turn heat off and let steep ten minutes more. Strain tea before serving.

BEEF JERKY (Sun-Dried)

Cut beef or venison with the grain in foot-long strips (no wider than 1/2"). Remove all fat. Dip strips into brine mixture of 1/4 cup salt to a gallon water. Dip til meat is no longer red and drain well. Coat meat strips in mixture of salt and coarse ground black pepper. Hang strips in sun. Use tree limbs, clothes line, or wire screen elevated from ground. (Sun and air must reach meat for drying process.) Screened meat may be covered with layer of cheesecloth. Strips must be turned to dry thoroughly. (Cover strips at night to prevent absorption of moisture.) Store in tightly-covered containers.

JERKY (Oven-Dried)

2 to 2¼ lbs. boneless MEAT (Beef, Veal, Venison)
1 cup WATER
2 tablespoons LIQUID SMOKE
¼ teaspoon PEPPER
1 teaspoon GARLIC SALT (optional)
½ teaspoon LEMON PEPPER (optional)

Trim fat from steak. Cut with grain into strips six inches long by 1/8 inch thick. Mix water, liquid smoke, salt and pepper (and optional ingredients). Marinate meat overnight in covered dish in refrigerator. Drain and dry thoroughly. Cover bottom rack of oven with aluminum foil; lay strips of meat close together (but not overlapping) on oven rack. Bake in slow oven (150 F to 175 F) overnight for 10 to 12 hours. (Beef should feel dry but not crisp.)Store in air-tight containers.

BEEFJERKY GRAVY

4 cups beef JERKY PIECES
3 tablespoons FAT
3 tablespoons FLOUR
2 cups MILK

With a heavy wooden mallet, pound jerky pieces into flakes and powder. Put pounded meat into heavy saucepan with fat. Over low heat, blend flour into fat. Cook and stir til flour has thickened. Continue cooking slowly, stirring constantly while adding milk. Cook over moderate heat, stirring til thickened. Serve on biscuits, potatoes, rice, or macaroni.

PEMMICAN

Jerked meat was often combined with beef suet to produce a trail food. Berries and wild fruits would be added to the mixture. This recipe substitutes honey as a binder and dried fruits for the jerked meat.

2 cups RAISINS
2 cups dry DATES
2 cups NUTS (or 1 cup dry cereal)
HONEY (for a binder)

Grind together all ingredients, except honey. Add honey (or suet) a little at a time, mixing well til moist enough to mold well and hold its shape. Pour into a pan til about 3/4 inch thick, or mold directly into bars. Refrigerate and cut individual bars from pan; wrap in aluminum foil.

QUAIL or PHEASANT

Remove pinfeathers from dressed birds and singe. Coat with flour and salt. Heat fat in heavy skillet and add birds, turning to brown on all sides. Add water to cover and bring to a boil. Cover and simmer til meat is tender.

NIXTAMAL (Partially-Cooked Corn)

1 gallon WATER
¼ cup unslaked LIME
8 cups dry (field) CORN

Mix water and lime in a galvanized container. Add corn and stir til bubbling stops. Cook (but do not boil) from one to two hours (til corn starts to peel). Remove from heat and let stand a day. Separate hulls from kernels and wash corn in several cold water rinses to remove lime traces. Drain and grind into masa.

MASA (Corn Dough)

Masa is ground corn dough (Nixtamal) used as the base for tortillas, tamales, and similar dishes. Masa Harina (which can be substituted for masa and reconstituted with water) is dehydrated nixtamal, and can be bought in grocery stores.

1 cup NIXTAMAL
WATER

Put a cup of nixtamal through a food chopper several times. Sprinkle with water while grinding to produce a medium-fine dough. Keep this corn dough covered to prevent drying.

ATOLE (Cereal)

1 cup MASA
2 cups cold WATER
¼ to ½ teaspoon SALT
3 cups boiling WATER

Mix masa slowly with cold water til lumps disappear, and add salt. Boil water in top of a double boiler, and slowly add the masa mixture (pouring slowly to prevent lumps). Cook on low flame for an hour, stirring often. Serve with cream and sugar or fresh fruit.

CORN TORTILLAS

2 lbs. MASA HARINA
2 teaspoons SALT

Mix masa harina well with water to form soft and pliable dough. Pinch off walnut-sized lump of dough between hands and shape into 6-inch circle (or use rolling pin or tortilla press). Place on heated, ungreased griddle til slightly brown; turn and brown other side.

PINOLE

Toast the nixtamal by spreading in heated, covered skillet and stirring occasionally 5 to 10 minutes. Grind coarsely to cereal consistency and serve cold with milk, sugar and cinnamon. Pinole may also be made by grinding chia seeds and other edible wild seeds, adding water, and cooking to a mush.

FLOUR TORTILLAS (Basic)

4 cups FLOUR (sifted)
2 teaspoons SALT
½ cup LARD (or fat)
1¼ to 1½ cups warm WATER

Measure flour into mixing bowl. Sprinkle in salt and mix well. Cut in lard (or fat) with two knives, pastry blender, or fingers. Add water slowly (mixing with fork or hands til ball of dough forms). Continue adding water til all flour is moistened. Knead in bowl (or on floured board) til dough is smooth (about 5 minutes) and pliable enough to stretch. With greased hands pinch off egg-sized balls of dough and set in bowl. Cover with cloth and let dough balls set from 15 minutes to half an hour. Shape dough balls into 6-inch circles by using rolling pin or patting with hand. (Flapping tortilla back and forth between hands helps keep it stretched.) Heat ungreased griddle or frypan and brown tortilla on one side (about 20-30 seconds). When dough begins to bubble, turn and brown other side. (Makes about 18 tortillas)

FLOUR TORTILLAS (Baking Powder)

4¼ cups FLOUR (sifted)
¾ tablespoon BAKING POWDER
½ cup LARD
1¼ tablespoons SALT
1¼ cups WATER (approx.)

Sift dry ingredients, cut in shortening and continue as above.

FRIJOLES (Beans)

For refried beans, the beans must be (1) boiled very dry and mashed, (2) fried and (3) refried.

½ lb. PINK BEANS
4 cups WATER
1 teaspoon SALT
1 teaspoon CHILI POWDER
¼ teaspoon crushed RED PEPPER
½ cup ONION (chopped)

Sort and wash beans. Add water, bring to a boil, cover tightly and cook two minutes. Remove from heat. Do not remove cover. Soak one hour. Add salt, chili powder, crushed red pepper and chopped onion. Bring to a boil, cover tightly, continue cooking slowly, stirring occasionally for two hours (or til beans are tender). Add more water, if needed, to keep beans from sticking. (Makes about 3 cups boiled beans.)

FRIJOLES FRITOS (Fried Beans)

Melt 1/2 cup lard in frypan and add 3 cups mashed beans. Fry, stirring over high heat til fat is mixed and beans are dry.

FRIJOLES REFRITOS (Refried Beans)

Melt 1/2 cup lard in frypan and add 3 cups fried beans. Fry, stirring over medium heat til fat is mixed and beans can be shaped into large patty. Sprinkle grated cheese over beans, turn over, cook a minute, turn again, so melted cheese is on top.

BEAN BURRITO

Burritos are flour tortillas wrapped around refried beans or chile con carne. To roll a burrito, use a 12-inch or 18-inch heated tortilla laid out flat. Fill with beans or chili and roll towards you. Fold sides in toward middle and set (seam down) on plate. Serve with shredded lettuce and sliced tomatoes.

TACOS

- ½ teaspoon FAT
- ½ lb. GROUND BEEF
- ½ teaspoon CUMINO SEED
- ½ clove GARLIC (mashed)
- 3 tablespoons FAT
- 6 corn TORTILLAS (soft and fresh)
- 1 TOMATO (sliced thin)
- ½ head LETTUCE (shredded)
- 1 teaspoon VINEGAR

(Two frypans needed). In one, heat fat, add beef and stir til meat loses red color. Grind cumino seed and garlic together, add 1/3 cup water and add to meat. Stir mixture and cook for five minutes, or til dry. In second frypan, melt remaining fat. Dip tortillas quickly into heated fat (til tortilla softens). (Tortillas can also be molded in a taco maker.) Set softened shells upright (with opening at top) in large bowl and fill with meat. Fry filled tortillas on each side in heated fat til crisp. (Tortillas may also be filled flat and folded over.) To serve: add few grains of salt to vinegar and 1/3 cup water. Sprinkle over tomatoes and lettuce and add vegetables to taco shells. Sprinkle grated cheese over filled taco and serve with sauce.

TACO HOT SAUCE

- 2 small cans TOMATO PASTE
- 1 to 1½ cups WATER
- ½ to 1 tablespoon crushed dry RED PEPPERS (Chile Tepins)
- ¼ cup White VINEGAR
- 1 teaspoon SALT
- 1 clove GARLIC (crushed)
- Pinch of OREGANO

Combine tomato paste and water in saucepan. Add remaining ingredients. Mix thoroughly, and simmer 1/2 an hour. To keep sauce a thin consistency, add water during simmering. Cool and serve with tacos. (Makes about 1 cup of sauce). (To intensify "hotness" of sauce, omit vinegar.)

ESTOFADO (Beef Stew)

- 1½ lbs. STEW BEEF (lean)
- 1 ONION (chopped)
- 1 clove GARLIC (chopped)
- ¼ cup OIL
- ½ cup TOMATO SAUCE
- 1 cup WATER
- 3 tablespoons wine VINEGAR
- 1 teaspoon SALT
- ½ teaspoon OREGANO
- ½ teaspoon PEPPER
- 3 large CARROTS (cut up)
- 3 large POTATOES (cut up)

Put all ingredients (except for carrots and potatoes) into a 2-quart covered pan. Cover and simmer over low heat for 1 1/2 to 2 hours. Add carrots and potatoes and continue simmering til meat is tender. (This stew will have a thin liquid.)

TAMALES

24 CORN HUSKS
2 lbs. TAMALE DOUGH
Tamale FILLING

Cover cornhusks with warm water and soak til softened; drain. Open husks individually and spread thin layer of tamale dough on smooth side of husk. Spread a tablespoon of meat filling down center of tamale dough. Fold filled husk into thirds lengthwise. (To prevent leaking from husk, prepare another husk with masa dough and wrap it around the first. Bottom and top of each husk will be unfilled; tie these ends with string.) Place tamales upright (or set them in layers) in a steamer, cover tightly, and steam for about 45 minutes. (Tamales are ready when husks pull away from tamale dough. Makes about one dozen.)

Tamale Dough

½ cup LARD
2 lbs. MASA
2 teaspoons BAKING POWDER
2 teaspoons SALT
¾ cup WATER

Beat lard til light and fluffy. Mix with masa and add baking powder and salt. Beat til mixture is fluffy (test by dropping spoonful into cup of cold water; masa dough should float to the top. If masa is too dry, add water and continue beating.)

Tamale Filling

¼ cup FLOUR
1 tablespoon FAT
¼ cup CHILI POWDER
½ cup TOMATO SAUCE
1 cup WATER
1 teaspoon SALT
2 cups CHICKEN (cooked and diced)

Heat fat and add flour to brown. Add chili powder and mix; add tomato sauce. Add water slowly and stir. Add salt and simmer til sauce is thickened. Add chicken (or shredded beef). Cool thoroughly before spreading on tamale dough.

TOSTADAS

¼ cup LARD
6 Corn TORTILLAS
2 cups BEANS (fried)
¼ cup CHEESE (grated)
LETTUCE (shredded)

Heat lard in frypan. Fry tortillas (turning with tongs) to cook evenly to a golden brown. Drain on paper towel. Cover the browned tostadas with hot beans, grated cheese and lettuce. (Serve immediately, or tostada loses crispness)

QUESADILLAS

1 cup JACK or LONGHORN CHEESE
4 tablespoons GREEN CHILI (chopped)
4 corn TORTILLAS

Sprinkle grated cheese and chili on half of a corn tortilla. Heat lard in frypan and slide tortilla into pan. When tortilla softens, fold in half, turn & fry other side. Drain and serve.

CHEESE ENCHILADAS

12 Corn TORTILLAS
1 ONION (chopped)
½ lb. JACK CHEESE (grated)

Heat fat; dip tortillas in and out of hot fat to soften; drain on paper towel. Dip tortillas in enchilada sauce. Place onion and cheese in center of tortilla. Roll up and place in baking dish. Top with remaining sauce and grated cheese. Set in 350 F oven (or in broiler) til cheese melts. Serve immediately.

Enchilada Sauce

2 tablespoons FLOUR
1 tablespoon BUTTER
½ teaspoon GARLIC POWDER
1 can RED CHILI SAUCE
1 cup WATER

Brown flour in butter, add chili sauce and bring to slow boil. Add garlic powder. Add water to thickness desired and simmer five minutes.

BEEF ENCHILADAS

¼ cup SHORTENING
1½ lbs. GROUND ROUND
1 ONION (chopped)
1 clove GARLIC (chopped)
3 tablespoons CHILI POWDER
1 can TOMATO SAUCE

Heat shortening. Add meat and fry til browned. Add onion, garlic and salt to taste. Combine 1/2 can tomato sauce with chili powder and add to meat. Mix thoroughly and add remaining tomato sauce. (Add water as needed for medium consistency.) Prepare enchiladas as directed above; spoon meat mixture into center of enchilada, roll, and bake (or broil).

SALSA de CHILI (Green Chili Relish)

2 cups TOMATOES (peeled and chopped)
1 stalk CELERY (diced)
1 ONION (diced)
1 GREEN PEPPER (diced)
1 teaspoon SALT
1 tablespoon white VINEGAR
2 teaspoons SUGAR
1 GREEN CHILI (chopped)

Combine vegetables, salt, vinegar, sugar and chili, and blend well. (For finer texture, put vegetables through fine blade of food grinder.) Cover and refrigerate overnight. Serve cold.

SALSA #2

1 can (No. 303) TOMATOES
1 can (small) GREEN CHILES
1 ONION (medium)
2 tablespoons VINEGAR
2 tablespoons OLIVE OIL

Grind tomatoes, chilis and onion; add vinegar and oil, dash of salt and pepper. Cover and refrigerate several hours.

CHILES RELLENOS (Stuffed Chiles)

8 fresh, frozen, or 2 cans GREEN CHILES (4 oz.)
1 lb. JACK CHEESE
4 EGG WHITES (stiffly beaten)
4 EGG YOLKS
FLOUR (as needed)
4 tablespoons LARD (or fat)
Grated CHEESE

(Peel fresh chili peppers by holding peppers on fork over open flame til skin blisters. Wrap peppers in damp towel to steam 10 minutes, or til papery skin peels off.) Split chiles lengthwise; remove seeds and membrane. Cut cheese into slices that will fit into the chile slits and overlap slit ends. Dip each stuffed chile into batter. (Prepare batter by beating egg whites til they peak; fold in beaten egg yolks and flour.) Heat fat in frypan and place coated chiles in pan. Heat for an instant and turn immediately. Fry til golden. Drain on paper towels. Place in baking dish, cover with sauce and top with grated cheese. Heat in 325 F oven til cheese melts (about 15 minutes).

Sauce

2 tablespoons LARD (or FAT)
2 ONIONS
3 cloves GARLIC
2 tablespoons FLOUR
1 can TOMATO PASTE (8 oz.)
½ cup WATER
½ teaspoon OREGANO (crumbled)
½ teaspoon SALT

Saute onions and garlic in hot fat til golden brown. Stir in flour; add tomato paste, water, oregano, and salt. Cook to consistency of gravy (about 15 minutes) and pour over chiles.

●

Chiles rellenos may be prepared ahead, fried, and stored in the refrigerator. When ready to use, add the sauce and grated cheese. Place in 325 F oven for 25 to 30 minutes.

SOPA de ALBONDIGAS (Meatball Soup)

Soup

1 ONION (minced)
1 clove GARLIC (minced)
2 tablespoons OIL
½ can TOMATO SAUCE
3 quarts BEEF STOCK
Sprig of MINT LEAVES

Meatballs

¾ lb. GROUND BEEF
¾ lb. GROUND PORK
1/3 cup raw RICE
1½ teaspoon SALT
¼ teaspoon PEPPER
1 EGG slightly beaten

Soup: Saute onion and garlic in oil. Add tomato sauce and beef stock and heat to boiling point.

Meatballs: Mix meat with rice, salt and pepper, and egg, and shape into little balls. Drop into boiling soup. Cover tightly and cook about 1/2 hour.

(Optional: add sprig of mint to broth about 10 minutes before soup has boiled, or add chopped mint leaves to meatballs.)

Dulces (Sweets)

FLAN (Caramel Custard)

1½ cups SUGAR
4 EGGS
1 can (14 oz.) CONDENSED MILK (not evaporated)
1 cup WATER
1 teaspoon VANILLA (or rum)

Caramelize sugar by pouring into heavy skillet and stirring frequently (with wooden spoon) over low flame, til sugar melts and turns golden. Pour sugar into 1-quart casserole, coating bottom and sides evenly. Allow sugar to cool and prepare custard: beat eggs, add milk, water, and vanilla. Pour into casserole and set casserole in a larger pan containing an inch of hot water. Bake in 350 F oven 1 to 1 1/2 hours (or til knife inserted in center comes out clean). Loosen with spatula and turn onto serving dish; chill and serve with sauce.

SOPAIPILLAS (Puffy Fritters)

1¾ cups sifted FLOUR
2 teaspoons BAKING POWDER
1 teaspoon SALT
2 tablespoons SHORTENING
2/3 cup cold WATER

Sift flour, baking powder and salt into mixing bowl. Add shortening, cut in coarsely. Add water gradually. Mix just enough to hold together as for pie crust. Turn out on lightly floured board and knead til smooth. Cover and let dough rest about five minutes. Roll out into 12 x 15 (dough should be very thin--about 1/8 inch thick). Cut into 3-inch squares; drop a few squares at a time into very hot oil. Turn squares over several times to make them puff evenly. Fry two or three minutes on each side, or til golden brown. Sopaipillas will puff up like tiny pillows. Serve with honey or cinnamon/sugar.

EMPANADAS (Baked Turnovers)

3 cups FLOUR
2 teaspoons BAKING POWDER
½ teaspoon SALT
½ cup SHORTENING
3 tablespoons SUGAR
½ cup MILK

Sift and mix dry ingredients. Cut in shortening. Add milk to hold dough together and beat. Roll dough on slightly floured board into 1/8-inch thickness. Cut into rounds (about a dozen). Fill with chili, taco meat, or fruit mixture (apple, pumpkin, or mince). Use about one to two tablespoons of filling for each turnover. Moisten dough edges with cold water. Fold empanada in half and seal edges together by pinching. Bake in 350 F oven 20-30 minutes. Sprinkle with confectioners sugar.

MEXICAN WEDDING CAKES

1 cup BUTTER (softened)
½ cup POWDERED SUGAR
1 teaspoon VANILLA
2¼ cups all-purpose FLOUR
¼ teaspoon SALT
1 cup NUTS (chopped fine)

Cream butter til light and fluffy. Add sugar and vanilla and mix thoroughly. Add flour, salt and nuts and mix well. Shape into walnut-sized balls (using about 1 teaspoon dough for each cake). Place balls on ungreased baking pan in 325 F oven for 20-30 minutes. (Cakes must not brown; do not overbake.) Roll in powdered sugar; cool, roll again in powdered sugar.

MEXICAN CHOCOLATE

1 stick CINNAMON
6 cups MILK
1 teaspoon VANILLA
6 squares CHOCOLATE (unsweetened, grated)
1 EGG (separated)

Put cinnamon stick in saucepan; add milk and vanilla; simmer and add chocolate when milk is warmed (not boiled). Add egg yolk and stir rapidly. Beat egg white til stiff and fold in. Serve at once. (Work rapidly to prevent egg from curdling). Sweeten to taste.

ALMENDRADO

1½ envelopes GELATIN
½ cup cold WATER
¼ cup boiling WATER
6 EGG WHITES
½ cup SUGAR
½ teaspoon VANILLA
½ teaspoon ALMOND EXTRACT
Pinch SALT
RED and GREEN FOOD COLORING

Soak gelatin in cold water. Add boiling water to dissolve. Cool. Beat egg whites stiff, but not dry. Add sugar gradually, alternating with gelatin liquid (using electric beater at high speed). Add vanilla, almond flavoring and salt. (Be sure to whip thoroughly so gelatin blends completely with egg whites.) Divide mixture into three parts. Leave one part white, tint other parts red and green (to resemble Mexican flag). Alternate layers by spooning into a loaf pan lined with waxed paper which extends above mixture. Chill at least 4 hours and serve with following custard.

Custard Sauce

2 tablespoons CORNSTARCH
1 tablespoon cold MILK
3 cups scalded MILK
½ cup SUGAR
Pinch of SALT
6 EGG YOLKS
½ teaspoon VANILLA
½ teaspoon ALMOND EXTRACT
Sliced, toasted ALMONDS

Dissolve cornstarch in cold milk, add to scalded milk, sugar and salt. Pour into saucepan and boil til slightly thickened, stirring constantly. Beat egg yolks, vanilla and almond flavoring. Add to hot mixture slowly, stirring constantly til slightly thickened (about a minute). Chill and serve by slicing almendrado and topping with custard sauce and almonds.

Sourdough

SOURDOUGH STARTER

To begin, take a glass jar or crock (nothing metal) and add:

1 cake (or 1 pkg.) YEAST
2 cups warm WATER
2 cups all-purpose FLOUR

Stir mixture to a smooth thin paste. Put on lid and set in a warm place to sour. Stir it several times a day; the sourdough should be ready in two or three days. (If no yeast is available, add 4 tablespoons sugar and 1 1/2 teaspoons salt to the starter, and it will sour, too, except the process will take five days.)

To keep starter active, add one cup unsifted flour and one cup warm water and let stand at room temperature either all night or all day. (Do this at least once a week.) Always reserve one-half cup or more of starter and store in refrigerator.

SOURDOUGH BREAD

1 quart SOURDOUGH
1 quart lukewarm WATER
¾ cup or 1 cup SUGAR
2 tablespoons SALT
6 tablespoons melted SHORTENING
12 cups FLOUR

Mix ingredients in order given (adding flour last), using enough flour to make a pliable dough. Knead til smooth and elastic. Place in a greased bowl and let rise. (Rising will take longer than yeast bread.) Knead down and let rise again. Shape into four oblong loaves and set on lightly-greased cooky sheet. Cover and set in warm place; let rise til almost double in size. Just before baking, brush outside with water; make diagonal slashes across tops with sharp knife. Bake in 350 F oven an hour.

SOURDOUGH ENGLISH MUFFINS

½ cup STARTER
1 cup MILK
2¾ cups FLOUR
1 tablespoon SUGAR
¾ teaspoon SALT
½ teaspoon SODA
CORNMEAL

In a large mixing bowl, combine starter, milk and two cups flour. Mix together, cover and set at room temperature about eight hours (or overnight). Mix 1/2 cup flour, sugar, salt and soda; sprinkle over dough; mix in thoroughly. Turn this very stiff dough out onto a board floured with remaining 1/4-cup flour. Knead about two or three minutes. Roll out to 3/4-inch thickness. Use a 3-inch cutter to cut nine muffins. Place one inch apart on cookie sheet. Cover with towel and let rise an hour. Sprinkle both sides with corn meal and bake in lightly-greased 300 F electric frypan with cover on for 10 minutes on each side. Split and serve hot with butter and honey or jam.

SOURDOUGH BISCUITS

1½ cups all-purpose FLOUR
2 teaspoons BAKING POWDER
¼ teaspoon BAKING SODA
½ teaspoon SALT
¼ cup melted BUTTER
1 cup STARTER

Sift dry ingredients together. Blend in butter and starter. Pat dough out on floured surface (adding more flour if necessary). Cut in rounds or squares and place on greased baking sheets. Cover and let rise 30 minutes (or til light). Bake in 425 F oven for 20 minutes or til browned. (Makes a dozen)

SOURDOUGH PANCAKES

½ cup SOURDOUGH STARTER
2 cups FLOUR
2 cups lukewarm WATER
2 level tablespoons SUGAR
1 teaspoon SALT
3 tablespoons melted SHORTENING
2 EGGS
1 teaspoon BAKING SODA

To the starter add flour and lukewarm water. Beat til smooth and let stand in a warm place overnight. Add sugar, salt and shortening. Beat in eggs. Dissolve soda in one tablespoon water and fold in gently. Do not stir after soda has been added. Grease griddle, pour out batter and flip once to brown.

SOURDOUGH BUCKWHEATS

Follow pancake recipe, but in place of the flour called for, substitute 1 1/2 cups buckwheat flour and 1/2 cup white flour.

SOURDOUGH CORN BREAD

1 cup SOURDOUGH STARTER
1½ cups YELLOW CORNMEAL
1½ cups EVAPORATED MILK
2 EGGS (beaten)
2 tablespoons SUGAR
¼ cup melted BUTTER (warm)
½ teaspoon SALT
About ¾ teaspoon SODA

Mix the starter, cornmeal, evaporated milk, eggs, and sugar thoroughly in a large bowl. Stir in butter, salt and soda. Turn into 10-inch greased pan and bake in 450 F oven 30 minutes.

SOURDOUGH MUFFINS

½ cup WHOLE WHEAT FLOUR
1½ cups WHITE FLOUR
½ cup melted SHORTENING
½ cup SUGAR
½ cup EVAPORATED MILK (do not dilute)
2 EGGS
1 cup RAISINS
1 teaspoon SALT
1 teaspoon SODA
½ cup SOURDOUGH

Combine all ingredients and stir only enough to blend. Bake in greased muffin pans in 425 F oven 25 minutes. (In place of evaporated milk, 1/2 cup water plus 2 tablespoons dry milk can be substituted.)

California Fruits

Mention fruit and one state pops to mind--California! Its area is so vast, its terrain so varied and its climate so vital that this golden state produces more fruit and more varieties of fruit than any other in the nation.

From the arid deserts of the Coachella Valley come dates as fine as any produced in Arabia or North Africa. Irrigated acreage of the Imperial Valley on the desert's edge produces sweet grapefruit and other citrus crops.

Oranges and other citrus fruit are grown in a wide belt of semi-tropical California, from San Diego and El Centro northward through Orange, Riverside, and Los Angeles County and on northward into the San Joaquin and Sacramento Valleys.

San Joaquin Valley vineyards support three major industries: table grape, wine and raisin. Figs, plums, apricots, nectarines, peaches, pears and other crops are also produced in this vast inland valley. Actually, grapes and many of these other fruits grow in various areas of California. Spanish mission grounds were the first to be planted with European grapes. Since that time they have flourished and provided California with the title of "The Nation's Vineyard" and a worldwide reputation for quality wines.

Avocado is a tropical fruit that loves California's warm southern coastal area from the Mexican border to Goleta. Today's avocado is descended from the ahuacatl of the Aztecs. The winter avocado is the green Fuerte, while summer brings the pebbled Hass variety (green to black).

Nuts were imported to America long before they were commercially planted on the west coast. Today, California is the world's leading producer of walnuts, and raises 95% of America's crop. Almonds, which are related to the plum and apricot, are presumed to have originated in China or the Middle East. Today, California is the only state where almonds are grown in commercial quantities.

Like so many other food crops that thrive on the west coast, the olive was brought to California by Spanish settlers. Olives are native to the Mediterranean perimeter, including Spain.

Strawberries are grown in every state, with the largest crop in California, grown primarily in the central part of the state, the counties of Santa Clara, Monterey and Santa Cruz.

LIME CHIFFON BANANA PIE

4 cups miniature MARSHMALLOWS
1/3 cup fresh LIME JUICE
4 EGGS (separated)
1 tablespoon LIME RIND
¼ cup SUGAR
2 BANANAS
1 (9 inch) GRAHAM CRACKER CRUST

Melt marshmallows and lime juice in double boiler top. Stir til smooth. Pour a small amount of heated mixture into slightly beaten egg yolks. Stir and combine with marshmallows. Cook from three to five minutes til thickened, stirring constantly. Add lime rind, mix well, and cool. Beat egg whites til frothy. Add sugar gradually. Continue beating til peaks form and fold into lime mixture. Slice bananas into crust. Pour lime mixture over bananas. Garnish with whipped cream and lime slices.

Graham Cracker Crust

1 2/3 cups Graham Cracker CRUMBS
¼ cup SUGAR
¼ cup BUTTER (softened)

Cover sides and bottom of 8-inch pie pan with crust and chill.

TANGERINE PIE

1 Graham Cracker CRUST
1 tablespoon unflavored GELATIN
¼ cup cold WATER
4 EGG YOLKS
¼ cup SUGAR
¾ cup TANGERINE JUICE
1 tablespoon LEMON JUICE
¼ teaspoon SALT
1½ teaspoon grated TANGERINE RIND
½ teaspoon grated LEMON RIND
4 EGG WHITES
¼ cup SUGAR
1/3 cup TANGERINE SECTIONS

Prepare crust in advance and chill several hours. Soften gelatine in cold water. Beat egg yolks in double boiler top til light. Beat in sugar gradually. Add tangerine juice, lemon juice, and salt. Cook over hot water, stirring often til thickened. Remove from heat. Add softened gelatin and rinds. Mix well, and cool til partially set. Beat egg whites til foamy. Add sugar gradually, beating constantly. Continue beating til soft peaks form. Fold beaten whites into tangerine mixture. Pour into crust and chill til set. Garnish with tangerine sections.

KUMQUAT RELISH

4 cups fresh CRANBERRIES (rinsed, drained)
4 APPLES (peeled, diced)
4 cups sliced fresh KUMQUATS
1½ cups SUGAR
1¼ cups white VINEGAR
2/3 cup WATER
12 whole CLOVES
3 CINNAMON STICKS

Combine all ingredients and simmer for 15 minutes (or til kumquats are translucent.) Spoon mixture while hot into sterilized jars. Seal with paraffin and cool. (Makes 4 pints)

ROSY CHICKEN

- 2 Coachella GRAPEFRUIT (peeled & sectioned)
- ½ cup APPLE CIDER
- 1 cup whole CRANBERRY SAUCE
- 1 tablespoon HONEY
- ¼ teaspoon CLOVES
- ¼ teaspoon SALT
- 1 FRYING CHICKEN (2½ lbs.) cut up
- 3 tablespoons BUTTER

Squeeze all juice from grapefruit membranes. Combine juice, cider, cranberry sauce, honey, cloves and salt. Heat to boiling; add grapefruit sections. Stir gently. Brown chicken in butter in frying pan. Remove to shallow baking pan. Baste with grapefruit sauce. Bake in 350 F oven about 45 minutes, basting occasionally with sauce. Remove chicken to platter. Drain fat from pan. Add remaining sauce to baking pan; stir to loosen browned bits. Bring to boil. Serve with chicken. (Serves 6)

TANGY TURKEY

- 3 large Coachella GRAPEFRUIT
- ½ teaspoon grated GRAPEFRUIT RIND
- ¼ cup GRAPEFRUIT JUICE
- ¼ cup BUTTER
- 1 cup GREEN PEPPER (in chunks)
- 2 cups TURKEY (cubed, cooked)
- 2 CHICKEN BOUILLON CUBES
- ½ cup boiling WATER
- ½ cup CHILI SAUCE
- ¼ cup WHITE WINE
- 2 teaspoons instant minced ONION
- ¾ teaspoon SALT
- 1/8 teaspoon PEPPER
- 1 tablespoon CORNSTARCH

Grate rind of grapefruit to make 1/2 teaspoon. Pare and section grapefruit. Squeeze juice from membranes to make 1/4 cup. Melt butter in a large skillet. Saute green pepper and turkey about 5 minutes, stirring occasionally. Meanwhile, dissolve bouillon cubes in boiling water. Add grapefruit rind and juice, chili sauce, wine, onion, salt, pepper and cornstarch; heat to boiling, stirring constantly til thickened. Turn into skillet over turkey. Add grapefruit sections and simmer gently five minutes. (Makes 4 servings)

GOLD RUSH COLESLAW

- 1 large head CABBAGE (shredded)
- 2 large ORANGES (peeled, bite size pieces)
- 1½ cups real MAYONNAISE
- 6 tablespoons SUGAR
- ¾ teaspoon DRY MUSTARD
- ¾ teaspoon CELERY SEED
- ½ teaspoon SALT
- ¼ teaspoon PEPPER
- 6 tablespoons freshly squeezed LEMON JUICE
- 1 tablespoon MILK (or cream)

Toss cabbage and orange pieces together in mixing bowl. Combine remaining ingredients, stirring til smooth. Pour over cabbage and toss lightly to mix well. Cover bowl with plastic wrap. Refrigerate for blending thirty minutes. Transfer chilled coleslaw to individual salad bowls with slotted spoon.

TANGERINE BRAN MUFFINS

1 cup whole bran CEREAL
1 cup MILK
1 tablespoon fresh grated TANGERINE PEEL
2 tablespoons fresh squeezed TANGERINE JUICE
1 EGG
¼ cup SALAD OIL
1¼ cups sifted FLOUR
3 teaspoons BAKING POWDER
¼ teaspoon BAKING SODA
½ teaspoon SALT
¼ cup SUGAR
1 TANGERINE (peeled, sectioned, seeded)

In mixing bowl, combine bran cereal and milk; let stand til most of moisture is absorbed. Add tangerine peel and juice, egg and oil; beat well. Resift flour with dry ingredients; add to bran mixture and stir just enough to blend. Spoon into greased muffin pans, filling about 3/4 full. Top each muffin with a tangerine section. Bake at 400 F for 30 minutes. (Makes 12 muffins)

MANDARIN MUFFINS

1 can (11 oz.) MANDARIN ORANGES
1½ cups all-purpose FLOUR
1¾ teaspoons BAKING POWDER
½ teaspoon each: SALT and NUTMEG
¼ teaspoon ALLSPICE
½ cup SUGAR
1/3 cup SHORTENING
1 EGG (slightly beaten)
¼ cup MILK
¼ cup melted BUTTER
¼ cup SUGAR mixed with ½ teaspoon CINNAMON

Drain mandarin oranges well and spread on paper towels. To mix batter, sift flour, measure, then sift with baking powder, salt, nutmeg, allspice and sugar into large bowl. Cut in shortening until mixture is in fine particles. Combine egg and milk and add all at once. Mix just til flour is moistened. Add the drained orange segments and mix lightly til evenly distributed. Spoon into large, greased muffin pans, filling 3/4 full. Bake for 20 minutes in 350 F oven. Remove from pans while hot and dip tops in melted butter, then roll in cinnamon-sugar. (Makes a dozen muffins)

LIME SNOW

2 envelopes unflavored GELATIN
1 cup cold WATER
½ cup SUGAR
1/8 teaspoon SALT
½ cup ice WATER
3 EGG WHITES
1 can (6 oz.) frozen LIMEADE CONCENTRATE (kept frozen)

Sprinkle gelatin over cold water in saucepan. Place over low heat and stir constantly til gelatin dissolves. Stir in sugar and salt. Add lime concentrate and ice water. Stir til melted. Chill til slightly thicker than consistency of unbeaten egg white. Add egg whites to gelatin mixture. Beat til mixture begins to hold its shape. Turn into mold and chill til firm. To serve: unmold and garnish with slices of lime.

Oranges

HONEY ORANGE BREAD

¼ cup BUTTER
1 cup mild flavored HONEY
1 EGG
1½ tablespoons grated ORANGE PEEL
2½ cups sifted all purpose FLOUR
2½ teaspoons BAKING POWDER
1 teaspoon SALT
¾ cup fresh ORANGE JUICE
¾ cup finely chopped WALNUTS

In large mixing bowl, cream butter. Continue creaming while adding honey in a fine stream. Add egg and beat. Add orange peel. Sift together dry ingredients. Add dry ingredients alternately with orange juice to creamed mixture. Beat til well-blended. Stir in nuts. Spoon batter into greased, lined 9x5x3 pan and bake in 325 F oven one hour (or til loaf tests done in center). Let stand 10 minutes; remove from pan. Cool on wire rack. Wrap in aluminum foil and store overnight.

ORANGE-BANANA BREAD

2½ cups sifted all purpose FLOUR
4 teaspoons BAKING POWDER
¾ teaspoon SALT
¾ cup chopped NUTS
1½ cups mixed CANDIED FRUITS
1/3 cup RAISINS
½ cup SHORTENING
¾ cup SUGAR
3 EGGS
½ cup mashed BANANA
½ cup ORANGE JUICE

Sift together flour,baking powder, and salt. Stir in chopped nuts, candied fruits, and raisins. Cream shortening, add sugar, beat til light and fluffy. Add eggs, one at a time, beating after each addition. Combine mashed bananas and orange juice. Add to creamed mixture alternately with flour mixture, beginning and ending with dry ingredients. Turn into greased, wax-paper lined 9x5x3 loaf pan. Bake at 350 F for 1 1/4 hours. Cool 20 minutes before turning out on cake rack.

ORANGE BISCUITS

¼ cup BUTTER
½ cup ORANGE JUICE
½ cup SUGAR
2 teaspoons grated ORANGE RIND
2 cups FLOUR
½ teaspoon SALT
3 teaspoons BAKING POWDER
3 tablespoons SHORTENING
¾ cup MILK
¼ cup SUGAR
½ teaspoon CINNAMON

Combine butter, orange juice, 1/2 cup sugar, and orange rind and cook two minutes. Pour into nine muffin pans. Sift flour, salt, and baking powder. Cut in shortening, and add milk. Stir til dough follows fork around bowl. Knead briefly and roll 1/4 inch thick. Sprinkle with sugar and cinnamon, and roll as jelly roll. Slice one-inch thick and place (cut side down) over orange mix in individual pans. Bake in 425 F oven 20-30 minutes.

ORANGE COFFEE CAKE

1 ORANGE (pulp & rind)
1 cup RAISINS
1/3 cup NUTS
2 cups FLOUR
1 teaspoon SODA
1 teaspoon SALT
1 cup SUGAR
½ cup SHORTENING
¾ cup MILK
2 EGGS (unbeaten)
¼ cup MILK

Juice orange and set juice aside. Grind together orange pulp and rind with raisins and nuts. In separate bowl, sift flour, soda, salt and sugar. Add shortening (room temperature) and milk. Beat two minutes. Add eggs and 1/4 cup milk. Beat two minutes. Fold in orange,raisin, nut mixture. Pour into well-greased, floured 13x9x2 pan and bake in 350 F oven 40-50 minutes. Cool in pan and spread with topping.

Topping

1/3 cup ORANGE JUICE
½ cup SUGAR
1 teaspoon CINNAMON
¼ cup NUTS (ground)

Drizzle orange juice over warm cake. Combine other ingredients and sprinkle over drizzled juice.

ORANGE MARMALADE

3 ORANGES
JUICE of 3 LEMONS
WATER and SUGAR

Wash and slice oranges paper thin. Dice slices and add lemon juice. Measure combined orange pulp and lemon juice; add an equal amount of cold water. Let stand uncovered 24 hours. Boil (uncovered) an hour. Let stand another 24 hours. Add an equal amount of sugar and boil again til jelly is formed (no longer than 10 minutes). Pour into hot, sterilized jelly glasses and cover with paraffin when slightly cooled. (Makes 8 glasses) (Clear marmalade depends on ripeness and tartness of fruit. When first ripe, fruit is richer in pectin and needs less cooking.)

CANDIED CITRUS PEEL

3 cups CITRUS PEEL (cut in strips)
(Oranges, Lemons, Grapefruit)
12 cups cold WATER
1½ cups SUGAR
½ cup HONEY
1 cup SUGAR

Wash fruit and score peel into quarters. Remove sections of peel with fingers; cut into uniform strips (about 3/8 inch wide). Put peel into cold water and boil (uncovered) 10 minutes. Drain and rinse. Repeat process with fresh water.

Combine 1 1/2 cups sugar, honey and boiling water; bring to a boil and boil one minute. Add cooked, drained peel and simmer briskly til almost all of syrup has been absorbed (about 30 to 40 minutes). Stir often to avoid sticking. Transfer peel to colander and drain thoroughly. Toss drained peel with remaining sugar in a large bowl, coating well. Spread pieces of peel out on waxed paper to dry. Store in tightly covered container.

GLAZED BAKED CHICKEN

2 FRYERS (cut for frying)

Orange Sauce

¾ cup fresh ORANGE JUICE
2 tablespoons fresh LEMON JUICE
¼ cup SALAD OIL
¼ cup HONEY
1 teaspoon SALT
½ teaspoon PEPPER
1 teaspoon DRY MUSTARD
½ teaspoon PAPRIKA

Place chicken pieces skin side down in a large mixing bowl. Pour sauce over chicken pieces and rotate to coat completely. Cover bowl and marinate in refrigerator for several hours (or overnight). Remove chicken from sauce and place, skin side down on rack in pan. (Line bottom of pan with foil to catch drippings.) Baste with sauce. Bake in 400 F oven for 30 minutes. Turn chicken and baste with remaining sauce. Bake 30 minutes more (or til done). If chicken browns too fast, cover with foil.

ORANGE RICE

¼ cup BUTTER
1 cup chopped CELERY
1 cup chopped GREEN ONIONS
1½ cups uncooked RICE
2 cups CHICKEN BROTH
1 1/3 cups ORANGE JUICE
2/3 cup RAISINS
1 tablespoon grated ORANGE PEEL
1 teaspoon SALT

Melt butter in baking pan or skillet. Add celery and onions and saute til tender. Stir in rice and continue cooking til rice is golden brown. Blend in chicken broth and orange juice. Heat to boiling. Stir in raisins, orange peel and salt. Cover with tight lid or foil. Bake at 350 F for 35 minutes. (Serves 6)

ORANGE-LEMON MOLD

3 envelopes unflavored GELATIN
1¼ cups COLD WATER
1 cup SUGAR
2 tablespoons grated ORANGE RIND
2 teaspoons grated LEMON RIND
1 cup fresh ORANGE JUICE
2/3 cup fresh LEMON JUICE
1 teaspoon VANILLA EXTRACT
1/8 teaspoon SALT
2 EGG WHITES
½ cup HEAVY CREAM (whipped)

Soften gelatine in 3/4 cup of cold water. Bring remaining water to boil and add to gelatine mixture. Mix well. Stir in 3/4 cup sugar, orange and lemon rinds, juice and vanilla. Chill til mixture begins to thicken. Add salt to egg whites til they stand up in soft peaks. Beat in remaining sugar. Fold into mixture with whipped cream. Turn into greased 6-cup mold and chill. To serve, unmold on serving platter and garnish.

ORANGE OATMEAL CAKE

1½ cups fresh ORANGE JUICE
1 cup old fashioned ROLLED OATS
½ cup BUTTER
1 cup WHITE SUGAR
½ cup BROWN SUGAR
2 EGGS
1 teaspoon VANILLA
1¾ cups sifted FLOUR
1 teaspoon BAKING POWDER
1 teaspoon SODA
½ teaspoon SALT
¼ teaspoon CINNAMON
1½ tablespoons grated ORANGE PEEL
½ cup chopped NUTS

Add oats to boiling orange juice. Set aside. Cream butter and sugars. Add eggs and vanilla, beating til fluffy. Sift together dry ingredients, and add alternately to creamed mixture with oats. Stir in orange peel and nuts. Pour into greased 9x13x2 pan and bake at 350 F for 35 minutes.

Orange Butter Frosting

½ cup packed BROWN SUGAR
¼ cup BUTTER
1 1/3 tablespoons grated ORANGE PEEL
1 tablespoon fresh ORANGE JUICE
1 cup shredded COCONUT
½ cup chopped NUTS

Combine sugar, butter, grated peel and orange juice in saucepan. Bring to boil and cook one minute, stirring constantly. Blend in remaining ingredients and spread on cooled cake.

CITRUS PLUM JELLY

5 lbs. Calif. RED PLUMS
6 ORANGES (peeled and sliced)
1 LEMON (sliced)
1 LIME (sliced)
SUGAR

Wash plums; cover with water in large pot. Add orange, lemon and lime slices and bring to boil. Reduce heat and simmer til plums are cooked and pulp separates from pits. Spread four layers of moistened cheesecloth over mixing bowl and secure with string. Pour fruit and liquid into cheesecloth, permitting fruit juices to drip through. Return juice to pot and boil 20 minutes. For every 4 cups of juice, add 3 1/2 cups sugar. Boil rapidly til jelly point is reached on candy or jelly thermometer. Pour into hot sterilized jars and seal at once. (Makes about 7 pints)

RUSSIAN TEA

3 cups boiling WATER
1/3 cup SUGAR
3 TEA BAGS
12 whole CLOVES
1 stick CINNAMON
1 strip fresh ORANGE PEEL
½ cup fresh ORANGE JUICE
3 tablespooons fresh LEMON JUICE

Pour boiling water over sugar, tea bags, spices and orange peel. Steep five minutes and strain. Stir in orange and lemon juices. Heat, but do not boil. Garnish with lemon cartwheels studded with whole cloves.

Lemons

SUPREME LEMON MERINGUE PIE

Unbaked 8" PIE SHELL
1 cup WATER
¾ cup SUGAR
¼ teaspoon SALT
1 teaspoon grated LEMON RIND
5 tablespoons CORNSTARCH (blended with ½ cup cold water)
3 EGG YOLKS (well-beaten)
1 tablespoon BUTTER
6 tablespoons LEMON JUICE

Combine water, sugar, salt and lemon rind in saucepan and bring to a boil. Add blended cornstarch and cook over low heat til thickened (about 5 minutes), stirring constantly. Remove from heat. Add separately the egg yolks, butter, and lemon juice (mixing well after each addition). Pour into 8'' baked or crumb pie shell. Top with meringue.

Meringue

3 EGG WHITES
¼ teaspoon CREAM of TARTAR
Dash of SALT
9 tablespoons SUGAR
1 teaspoon LEMON JUICE

Beat egg whites stiff (but not dry). Sprinkle cream of tartar and salt over whites and beat lightly. Add sugar slowly by tablespoons (beating thoroughly to dissolve sugar grains. Fold in lemon juice and swirl meringue on pie, bringing to outer rim of pastry (to prevent shrinkage). Bake in 325 F oven 15 minutes (on middle shelf). Open oven door slightly and allow pie to cool slowly. While meringues are slightly warm, cut through meringues only with heated knife; chill and serve.

LEMON VELVET PIE

1 can (14 oz.) CONDENSED MILK (not evaporated)
6 tablespoons LEMON JUICE
Grated RIND of 1 LEMON
2 EGG YOLKS (beaten)

Combine milk, lemon juice and grated rind; add eggs and stir til thoroughly mixed. Pour into 8'' baked or crumb shell. Top with meringue, brown, and chill thoroughly before serving.

LEMON MARMALADE

6 unpeeled LEMONS (thinly sliced, cut crosswise and diced)

Measure diced fruit, and add three times as much water. Boil til tender (about 15-20 minutes). Replace liquid boiled away with water. Measure fruit juice and allow 3/4 cup sugar to each cup juice. Cook in 2-cup batches (about 10 minutes or til mixture drops thickly from spoon). Pour into sterilized glasses and cover with paraffin. (Makes eight 6-oz. glasses)

LEMON CAKE PUDDING

2 tablespoons FLOUR
¾ cup SUGAR
1 tablespoon BUTTER
2 EGG YOLKS (beaten)
¼ cup LEMON JUICE
1 cup MILK
2 EGG WHITES (stiffly beaten)

Cream flour, sugar and butter. Add egg yolks, lemon juice and milk and beat til smooth. Fold in egg whites. Pour into 8-inch square baking dish or individual custard cups. Set in pan of warm water and bake in 350 F to 375 F oven for 30 to 35 minutes. (Forms a cake top pudding with custard below).

LEMON CHEESE CAKE

1½ cups ZWIEBACK CRUMBS (about 19 slices)
2 tablespoons SUGAR
¼ cup BUTTER (melted)
1 lb. COTTAGE CHEESE
¼ cup CORN STARCH
4 EGGS (separated)
1 cup SUGAR
1¼ tablespoons LEMON JUICE
1½ teaspoons grated LEMON PEEL
½ teaspoon VANILLA
¼ teaspoon SALT
1 cup CREAM (whipped)

Blend zwieback crumbs, sugar and butter to fine consistency. Press 3/4 of mixture on bottom and sides of lightly greased 9-inch spring form pan. Bake in 325 F oven 5 minutes and cool. Put cottage cheese through strainer twice. Add corn starch and beat with spoon til fluffy. Beat whites til stiff (but not dry). Beat yolks slightly, add 1/2 cup sugar and beat til thick. Mix in lemon juice and peel, vanilla and salt. Fold in cheese mixture and then whipped cream. Fold remaining sugar into beaten egg whites. Then fold into cheese mixture slowly, but thoroughly. Pour batter into spring form pan. Sprinkle with remaining crumb mixture. Bake in 325 F oven 50 to 60 minutes. Turn off oven. Let cheese cake remain in oven til firm (about 45 more minutes). Cool completely before removing from pan.

LEMON SUGAR COOKIES

2 cups FLOUR
1 teaspoon BAKING POWDER
½ teaspoon SALT
½ cup BUTTER
1 cup SUGAR
1 EGG
1 tablespoon grated LEMON RIND
1 tablespoon LEMON JUICE

Combine and sift flour, baking powder and salt. Cream butter and add sugar, egg, lemon rind and juice. Beat til light and fluffy. Add dry ingredients and stir til completely mixed. Wrap dough in plastic, chill in refrigerator. Roll 1/8 thick on lightly floured board. Cut into rounds with cooky cutter and place on ungreased baking sheet. Sprinkle with sugar and bake in 375 F oven til edges are delicately browned (about 8 minutes). Remove from pan and cool on wire rack. (Makes 36 cookies)

LEMONY LOAF

2¼ cups FLOUR
2 teaspoons BAKING POWDER
¼ teaspoon SALT
½ cup SHORTENING
2/3 cup SUGAR
2 EGGS
1 cup MILK
2 teaspoons grated LEMON RIND
½ cup chopped WALNUTS
1 tablespoon LEMON JUICE

Sift and measure flour. Sift again with baking powder and salt. Cream shortening with sugar. Add (one at a time) eggs, beating well after each addition. Add flour to egg mixture in thirds, alternating with milk. Stir in lemon rind, nuts, and lemon juice. Blend quickly and spoon into well-greased 5x8 1/2 loaf pan. Bake in 350 F oven for an hour (or til brown and firm in center). Remove from oven and let stand in pan five minutes. Remove from pan and set on rack. Brush glaze on top of loaf with a pastry brush. Cover top of loaf completely (cake will absorb some of glaze). Cool, then wrap and store in refrigerator or freezer.

Lemon Glaze

3 tablespoons fresh LEMON JUICE
1/3 cup POWDERED SUGAR

Combine ingredients and use pastry brush to glaze loaf.

FANCY LEMON SPONGE CAKE

2¼ cups sifted CAKE FLOUR
1½ cups SUGAR
1 tablespoon BAKING POWDER
1 teaspoon SALT
½ cup OIL
6 EGGS (separated)
¾ cup cold WATER
2 teaspoons fresh LEMON JUICE
½ teaspoon grated LEMON RIND
½ teaspoon CREAM OF TARTAR

Sift together flour, sugar, baking powder, salt. Make a well in the dry ingredients, add oil, egg yolks, water, juice and rind. Beat vigorously with spoon til smooth. Add cream of tartar to egg whites. Beat til stiff. Pour the yolk mixture over the whites gradually. Fold carefully til just blended. DO NOT STIR. Pour immediately into ungreased 10x4 tube pan. Bake in 325 F oven for 70 minutes. Cool five minutes in pan and remove to cooling rack.

Fluffy Lemon Frosting

½ cup BUTTER
Dash SALT
4 cups sifted POWDERED SUGAR
3 tablespoons LEMON JUICE
2 teaspoons LEMON RIND

Cream butter and add salt. Add few tablespoons of sugar to creamed mixture and continue creaming. Add remaining sugar alternately with lemon juice and rind. Continue creaming til light and fluffy. Spread carefully over cooled cake.

Peaches

LAMB STEAKS WITH PEACHES

6 shoulder LAMB STEAKS
2 tablespoons VEGETABLE OIL
1 ONION (minced)
1½ cup TOMATO SAUCE
½ cup VINEGAR
¼ cup WATER
3 tablespoons LIGHT BROWN SUGAR (firmly packed)
1 tablespoon WORCESTERSHIRE SAUCE
2 teaspoons SALT
6 fresh Calif. PEACHES (peeled and sliced)

In a large skillet, brown steaks on both sides in oil. Remove steaks to platter. Add onion to skillet and cook until soft. Add remaining ingredients (except peaches) and stir to blend. Return steaks to skillet; spoon some sauce over. Cover pan. Simmer over low heat, turning occasionally, about an hour, or til steaks are tender. Add peaches and simmer 5 minutes more. Serve at once.

PERSIAN PEACH GLAZED CHICKEN

1 roasting CHICKEN (about 6 lbs.)
SALT
3 large fresh Calif. PEACHES (peeled and diced)
¼ cup SUGAR
Juice and rind of 1 ORANGE
2 tablespoons minced crystallized GINGER
1 teaspoon CURRY POWDER
1 tablespoon finely chopped ONION
1 tablespoon AROMATIC BITTERS
MINT Sprigs
Fresh Calif. PEACH Slices

Wash chicken; pat dry. Sprinkle with salt. Roast at 350 F for 2 1/2 hours. Combine remaining ingredients and simmer til thick and jam-like. Brush chicken heavily with glaze and continue roasting about 30 minutes longer til chicken is tender (being careful not to burn glaze). Garnish with fresh mint and slices of peeled fresh peach. (Makes 6 servings)

MEDITERRANEAN della ROBBIA

1 pkg. (3¼ oz.) VANILLA PUDDING MIX
1¾ cups MILK
¼ cup ORANGE FLAVORED LIQUEUR
3 fresh Calif. PLUMS (halved)
2 fresh Calif. PEACHES (peeled and sliced)
1 fresh Calif. Bartlett PEAR (halved, cored)
1 cup seedless GRAPES
½ cup CURRANT JELLY (melted over heat)

Prepare pudding as package directs; use only 1 3/4 cups milk. Remove from heat; stir in liqueur. Pour into shallow bowl and chill until set. Arrange fruit on pudding. Drizzle melted jelly over fruit and chill. (Makes 6 servings)

STUFFED PEACH PIE

PASTRY for one-crust pie
1 cup crushed MACAROONS
6 fresh Calif. PEACHES
½ cup BROWN SUGAR (firmly packed)
¼ cup chopped WALNUTS
2 tablespoons MAPLE SYRUP
NUTMEG SAUCE

Preheat oven to 425 degrees. Prepare favorite pie pastry and set aside. Crush macaroons and place in bottom of an 8-inch pie plate. Peel, halve and remove stones from peaches. In a small bowl, combine brown sugar, walnuts and syrup, mixing thoroughly. Place a heaping teaspoon of the brown sugar mixture in six peach halves. Gently press other halves on top of stuffed halves. Arrange in pie plate. Roll out pastry and place on top of peaches. Bake in preheated oven for 20 minutes (or til pastry is lightly browned). Serve with Nutmeg Sauce.

Nutmeg Sauce

1 cup SUGAR
1 tablespoon FLOUR
1 cup BOILING WATER
1 tablespoon BUTTER
1 teaspoon NUTMEG
1 tablespoon fresh LEMON JUICE

Combine sugar and flour together in a saucepan. Add boiling water and cook, stirring constantly til sauce thickens slightly. Add butter and simmer gently for 5 minutes. Remove from heat and stir in nutmeg and lemon juice. Serve warm.

PEACHES 'N CREAM PIE

Pastry

TWO-CRUST 9" PIE SHELL

2 cups sifted FLOUR
1 teaspoon SALT
6 tablespoons BUTTER
6 tablespoons SHORTENING
4 to 6 tablespoons ICE WATER

In a mixing bowl combine flour and salt. Cut in butter and shortening with pastry blender. Add ice water and stir with a fork until dough forms a ball. Chill.

Peachy Filling

6 fresh Calif. PEACHES (peeled and sliced)
½ cup SUGAR
3 tablespoons FLOUR
Dash SALT
½ teaspoon NUTMEG
½ cup WHIPPING CREAM
½ teaspoon VANILLA

Preheat oven to 450 F. Roll out 1/2 pastry to line 9-inch pie plate. Fill shell with peaches. In small bowl combine remaining ingredients; pour over peaches. Roll out remaining pastry; put over top of pie and crimp edges. Slash top; bake 10 minutes. Reduce heat to 350 F and continue baking 45 to 50 minutes. Serve warm or cool with ice cream. (Makes 6 servings)

CHINESE PEACH MARMALADE

3 lbs. fresh Calif. PEACHES (peeled and chopped)
Skin of 1 ORANGE (cut into thin strips)
Skin of 1 LIME (cut into thin strips)
Juice from 1 ORANGE
Juice from 1 LIME
Juice from 1 LEMON
2 tablespoons freshly grated GINGER ROOT (or 1½ teaspoons ground ginger)
3 lbs. SUGAR (9 cups)

Combine all ingredients in a heavy kettle and bring to a boil. Cook, stirring constantly, for one hour or until thickened to the consistency of marmalade. Ladle into hot, sterilized jars and seal at once. (Makes 2 pints)

SWEET 'N SOUR PICKLED PEACHES

4 lbs. small fresh Calif. PEACHES (approx. 12 peaches)
CLOVES (4 for each peach)
4 lbs. BROWN SUGAR
3 cups WHITE VINEGAR

Place peaches in boiling water for 30 seconds. Remove with slotted spoon; run under cold water and remove skins. Insert cloves. Mix sugar and vinegar in large kettle and bring to a boil, stirring til sugar has dissolved. Add peaches. Cover and poach four minutes. Remove peaches with slotted spoon and set aside. Cook syrup, uncovered, 10 minutes. Add the peaches and cook 2 minutes more. Fill sterilized jars with peaches and pour boiling syrup over them. Seal tightly. (Makes 4 pints)

PEACH SKILLET PIE

8 cups fresh Calif. PEACHES (sliced)
1 cup SUGAR
1/3 cup FLOUR
1 tablespoon LEMON JUICE
½ teaspoon NUTMEG
¼ teaspoon ALMOND EXTRACT
1 pkg. (11 oz.) PIE CRUST MIX
3 tablespoons BUTTER

Preheat oven to 400 F. Combine peaches, sugar, flour, lemon juice, nutmeg and extract. Prepare pie crust mix as package directs. Roll out on floured board to 20-inch square. Trim edges straight; save trimmings. Place crust in 10-inch square skillet or baking pan; allow corner of crust to hang over each side. Fill with peaches; dot with butter. Fold corners of crust over. Reroll trimmings and cut out leaves. Place along edges of crust, securing with water. Bake 50 to 55 minutes. (Makes one 10-inch square pie.)

PEACHES 'n BEANS

Mix two tablespoons any fruit juice with two tablespoons brown sugar in pan and heat. Add six peeled peach halves; sprinkle with cinnamon. Cook over low heat, turning peaches several times til well coated. Add 1-lb. can pork and beans and heat thoroughly.

Pears

FRANCISCAN POT ROAST

1 BEEF POT ROAST (4 to 5 lbs.)
2 cups WATER
¾ cup RED WINE
1/3 cup CATSUP
1½ to 2 teaspoons SALT
¼ teaspoons PEPPER
½ BAY LEAF (crushed)
8 CARROTS (whole or halved)
4 or 5 fresh Calif. Bartlett PEARS
Whole CLOVES
2 tablespoons CORNSTARCH
2 tablespoons WATER

Brown meat in covered pot. Mix water, wine, catsup, salt, pepper and bay leaf and pour over meat. Bring to boil, reduce heat, cover and simmer 2 to 2 1/2 hours (til almost tender). Add carrots and cook covered 30 minutes more. Pare, halve and core pears; stud each half with 3 cloves. Remove meat and carrots to platter; keep warm. Skim fat from stock. Add pears. Cook, turning as needed, 6 to 8 minutes til tender. Mix cornstarch and water. Stir into stock and cook, stirring, til slightly thickened. Arrange pears on platter with meat and carrots. Serve sauce in bowl. (Makes 8 servings)

MINT SAUCE PEAR DESSERT

2 fresh Calif. Bartlett PEARS
½ cup MINT JELLY
1 tablespoon CORNSTARCH
1/3 cup WATER
1½ teaspoons grated ORANGE RIND
¼ cup CREME DE MENTHE LIQUEUR
Dash SALT
6 servings VANILLA ICE CREAM (meringue shells or rice pudding)

Pare, halve and core pears. Cut each half lengthwise into 4 slices. Melt jelly; blend in cornstarch mixed with water. Cook and stir until thickened. Add rind, liqueur and salt; mix well. Add pear slices; heat 2 or 3 minutes. Spoon over ice cream, meringues or pudding. (Makes 6 servings)

PUNCHY PEAR CRISP

4 fresh Calif. Bartlett PEARS
¼ cup HONEY
½ teaspoon VANILLA
2 tablespoons ROLLED OATS
2 tablespoons WHEAT GERM
2 tablespoons BROWN SUGAR
2 tablespoons BUTTER

Wash and core pears; quarter and slice thin. Toss with honey and vanilla in buttered baking dish. Combine oats, wheat germ, sugar and butter; mix with fork to crumbled consistency. Pat lightly over pears. Bake at 350 F about 40 minutes, until top is lightly browned. Serve warm or cooled with sour cream, whipped cream, or ice cream. (Makes 6 servings)

MINTED PEARS MANDARIN

Combine pear slices and mandarin orange slices in chilled dessert dishes. Top with crushed ice and green creme de menthe.

BARTLETT BREAD PUDDING

3 or 4 fresh Calif. PEARS
¼ cup LEMON JUICE
2 cups stale BREAD CUBES
1/3 cup melted BUTTER
¼ cup SUGAR
½ teaspoon SALT
¼ teaspoon ALLSPICE
¼ teaspoon CINNAMON
½ cup RAISINS

Pare, halve and core pears; dice to measure 3 cups. Mix with lemon. Mix bread, butter, sugar, salt and spices. Place 1/2 of the combination in buttered 1 1/2 quart casserole. Top with pears, raisins and remaining bread. Bake covered at 350 F 15 minutes. Uncover; bake 20 minutes longer. Serve with whipped cream or vanilla ice cream. (Makes 4 servings).

PEAR CARAMEL CRUNCH PIE

5 fresh Calif. Bartlett PEARS
Unbaked pastry for 9" PIE SHELL
1 tablespoon FLOUR
1 tablespoon LEMON JUICE
1 cup BROWN SUGAR (firmly packed)
1½ cups crushed CORN FLAKES
1/3 cup BUTTER
1 teaspoon CINNAMON

Pare, halve, core and slice pears. Line 9-inch pie plate with pastry; flute edges. Sprinkle flour on pie shell. Arrange pears over and sprinkle with lemon juice. With pastry blender (or 2 knives) mix all remaining ingredients and spread over pears. Bake at 375 F 45 to 50 minutes, until pears are fork tender and top is crisp and lightly browned. Serve warm.

PEAR-PEANUT BUTTER SQUARES

1 fresh Calif. Bartlett PEAR
1/3 cup granulated SUGAR
1/3 cup BROWN SUGAR (firmly packed)
1/3 cup BUTTER
1/3 cup PEANUT BUTTER
1 EGG
¾ cup sifted all purpose FLOUR
¼ teaspoon BAKING POWDER
½ teaspoon SODA
¼ teaspoon SALT

Pare, halve, core and mash pear; cream with sugars, butter, peanut butter and egg. Sift remaining ingredients together into creamed mixture; mix well. Pour into greased 9 x 9 pan and bake at 350 F for 25 minutes. Cool. Cut into 2 1/4 inch squares. (Makes 16 squares)

PEAR PRALINE SPICY CAKE

1 pkg. (1 lb. 2½ oz.) SPICE CAKE MIX
2 fresh Calif. Bartlett PEARS
¼ cup melted BUTTER
½ cup BROWN SUGAR
2 tablespoons FLOUR
2 tablespoons WATER
¼ cup roasted diced ALMONDS

Prepare cake as package directs. Bake in 13x9x2 pan. Pare, halve, core and thinly slice pears. Arrange on top of hot cake. Mix remaining ingredients; spoon over pears. Broil 3 inches from heat til pears are thoroughly heated and topping is bubbly.

Plums

SUMMERY PLUM SALAD

4 fresh Calif. PLUMS (sliced)
1 cup seedless GRAPES
1 cup sliced fresh STRAWBERRIES
1 cup cubed CANTALOUPE
Juice of 1 LEMON
½ cup ORANGE JUICE
¼ cup WHITE WINE
¼ teaspoon TARRAGON
1 BANANA (peeled and sliced)

Combine first four ingredients in a bowl. Toss lightly with lemon juice. Combine orange juice, wine and tarragon, pour over fruit and marinate two to three hours. Add banana just before serving. (Makes 4 servings)

PLUM GOOD HAM

1 canned HAM (5 lbs.)
1 teaspoon DRY MUSTARD
½ teaspoon CLOVES
2 tablespoons CORNSTARCH
1/3 cup LEMON JUICE
½ cup WATER
1/3 cup SUGAR
8 fresh Calif. PLUMS (diced)

Preheat oven to 350 F. Cut ham in half (lengthwise) and rub with mustard and cloves. Place half in baking pan. Mix cornstarch, lemon, water and sugar. Cook, stirring til thickened. Add plums; simmer til tender. Spoon half the sauce on ham. Top with other half of ham and remainder of sauce. Bake an hour. (Makes 12 servings)

PETER PIPER PICKLED PLUMS

5 lbs. fresh Calif. PLUMS
3 cups WHITE VINEGAR
5 cups SUGAR
12 whole CLOVES
1 tablespoon MIXED PICKLING SPICES
4 cups WATER

Wash plums and place in one-gallon jug or crock. In large kettle, combine vinegar, sugar, cloves, pickling spices and water. Bring to boil and boil 15 minutes. Remove from heat and pour over plums. Refrigerate, covered, 3 to 5 days. (Makes about 2 quarts)

PLUM CUPS

4 cups BISCUIT MIX
1/3 cup SUGAR
2 EGGS
1½ cups MILK
2 tablespoons OIL
9 fresh Calif. PLUMS (halved)
1/3 cup SUGAR
2 teaspoons CINNAMON

Preheat oven to 400 F. Combine biscuit mix, sugar, eggs, milk and oil. Stir until blended but still lumpy. Grease muffin pans; fill 2/3 full. Put plums cut-side down on batter. Sprinkle with cinnamon-sugar. Bake 20 to 25 minutes. Remove from pans and cool on rack. (Makes 18 muffins)

PLUM DUMPLINGS

3 cups FRUIT JUICE
¾ cup SUGAR
2 cups BISCUIT MIX
2/3 cup MILK
6 fresh Calif. PLUMS (halved and pitted)
1 tablespoon LEMON JUICE
½ cup melted BUTTER
1 cup BROWN SUGAR

Mix juice and sugar in saucepan. Bring to boil; simmer five minutes. Set aside. Mix biscuit mix and milk with fork. Turn onto well-floured board and knead 5 times. Pat out to 1/2-inch thickness. Cut into 12 squares. Put plum half on each square. Pinch closed and roll into round ball. Lower one at a time into simmering syrup and cook 3 minutes. Turn dumpling over, cover pan and simmer 5 minutes more. Remove with slotted spoon to serving plates. Drizzle lemon juice over dumplings, then butter. Sprinkle with brown sugar. Serve warm with fruit syrup. (Makes 6 servings)

CHINESE PLUM SAUCE for SpareRibs

1 medium ONION (cut in wedges)
1 tablespoon VEGETABLE OIL
2 tablespoons CORNSTARCH
¾ cup VINEGAR
¾ cup SUGAR
2 lbs. fresh Calif. PLUMS (quartered)
½ teaspoon SALT
¼ teaspoon ALMOND EXTRACT

In saucepan cook onion until soft. Mix cornstarch with vinegar and sugar; add to onion. Cook, stirring until thickened. Add plums, salt and extract. Continue cooking until fruit is tender. Spoon some sauce over partially-cooked spareribs. Grill, brushing frequently with sauce. Heat remaining sauce to serve with barbecued spareribs. (Makes about 2 1/2 cups)

DEEP DISH PLUM PIE

1 cup SUGAR
½ cup FLOUR
½ teaspoon CINNAMON
½ teaspoon NUTMEG
Grated rind of 1 ORANGE
8 cups sliced, pitted fresh Calif. PLUMS
3 tablespoons BUTTER
1 pkg. PIE CRUST MIX

Combine sugar, flour, cinnamon, nutmeg, orange rind and plums and toss to coat plum slices. Pour mixture into a well-greased, 2-quart casserole. Dot top with butter. Prepare pie crust mix according to package directions. Roll out pie crust on a floured board large enough to cover the top of the casserole and allow an inch overhang. Place crust over plums and crimp edges. Slash top. Bake in a preheated oven (425 F) for one hour. (Place casserole on a cookie sheet to catch overflow of juice). Serve warm or cold spooned into bowls topped with small scoop of vanilla ice cream.

FRESH PLUM FREEZE

2 cups fresh Calif. PLUMS (sliced)
Juice of 1 LEMON
Juice of 1 ORANGE
Dash of SALT
¾ cup SUGAR
2 cups MILK

In a blender, combine all ingredients and puree until smooth. Pour mixture into ice cube tray and freeze until outer edges are firm but center is slushy. Transfer to chilled bowl and beat til smooth. Return to ice cube tray and freeze til firm. Serve with Cinnamon Plum Sauce. (Makes 4 servings)

Cinnamon Sauce

1 lb. fresh Calif. PLUMS (sliced)
1 cup SUGAR
1 stick CINNAMON
1 tablespoon CORNSTARCH
2 tablespoons LEMON JUICE
2 tablespoons WATER

In a saucepan, mix plums with sugar and let stand to form juices. Add cinnamon stick; simmer gently til fruit is tender (about 10 minutes). Mix cornstarch with lemon juice and water; stir into sauce. Cook, stirring til sauce thickens. Chill and serve over plum freeze, ice cream or pudding.

RASPBERRY/PLUM BUTTER

2 lbs. fresh Calif. PLUMS (quartered)
1 pkg. (10 oz.) frozen RASPBERRIES (thawed)
1 cup WATER
2½ cups granulated SUGAR
2 tablespoons LEMON JUICE

Combine plums, thawed raspberries, with liquid, and water in a heavy kettle. Bring to a boil, reduce heat and cook til fruit is very tender. Remove from heat and puree in blender. Return puree to kettle and add remaining ingredients. Cook over low heat til sugar is dissolved. Increase heat, and, stirring constantly, cook til butter is thick and glossy. (Butter is ready for canning when it sheets from a spoon. Another test for butter consistency is to drop a spoonful on a plate--if no rim of liquid forms around the edge of the butter, it's ready to be poured into sterilized jars). Seal while hot. (Makes 2 pints)

APPLE/PLUM BUTTER

2 lbs. fresh Calif. PLUMS (quartered)
2 lbs. APPLES (cored and quartered)
2 cups WATER
2¾ cups granulated SUGAR
2 teaspoons CINNAMON
1 teaspoon NUTMEG
¼ teaspoon ALLSPICE

Combine plums, apples and water in heavy kettle. Follow directions for Raspberry-Plum Butter, substituting apples for berries. (Makes 3 pints)

Nectarines

SHORT RIBS DINUBA

4 to 4½ lbs. BEEF SHORT RIBS
1 tablespoon SALAD OIL
2 cups APPLE JUICE (or water)
¼ cup finely chopped ONION
1 teaspoon SALT
½ teaspoon coarsely ground PEPPER
½ teaspoon WHOLE ALLSPICE
2 BAY LEAVES
2 or 3 fresh Calif. NECTARINES
1 tablespoon FLOUR
¼ cup WATER
1 cup dairy SOUR CREAM

Have butcher cut short ribs into serving-size pieces. In a Dutch oven over medium-high heat, brown short ribs on all sides in oil. Stir together apple juice, onion, salt, pepper, allspice and bay leaves; pour over meat. Cover and cook over low heat about two hours, til meat is tender. Slice nectarines to make about two cups; arrange over meat, cover and simmer 15 minutes longer. Remove meat and fruit to serving plate; keep warm. Combine flour and water; stir into pan liquid. Cook, stirring, until thickened. Blend in sour cream. Strain into bowl and serve as gravy. (Makes 4 servings)

CHICKEN 'N NOODLES NECTARINE

2 BROILER FRYERS (halved), (about 2 lbs. each)
¼ cup CATSUP
¼ cup WATER
¼ cup melted BUTTER
¼ cup dry SHERRY (or apple juice)
2 tablespoons TARRAGON VINEGAR
2 teaspoons SOY SAUCE
3 fresh Calif. NECTARINES
½ lb. SPINACH NOODLES
1 can (5 oz.) WATER CHESTNUTS (drained)
½ cup chopped GREEN ONION
SALT and PEPPER

Wash chicken; pat dry. Arrange in 13x9x2 baking pan. Mix catsup, water, butter, sherry, vinegar and soy; pour over chicken. Marinate several hours, turning often. Bake skin-side down at 425 F for 25 minutes, basting often with sauce. Turn chicken halves and baste; bake 35 minutes longer until tender. Meanwhile, dice nectarines to measure 2 1/2 cups. Cook the noodles as package directs; drain. Spoon sauce from chicken over noodles; fold in nectarines, chestnuts, onion, salt and pepper. Heat through. Turn onto hot platter; arrange chicken on top and serve at once. (Makes 4 servings)

CHERRY NECTARINE DREAM

Prepare one 3-oz. pkg. cherry flavor gelatin. Chill til slightly thickened. Stir in one pint vanilla ice cream. Beat one minute at high speed. Fold in two fresh California nectarines, diced. Spoon into chilled dessert glasses; refrigerate til ready to serve.

NECTARINE BETTY

4 cups fresh Calif. NECTARINES (sliced)
½ cup BROWN SUGAR (firmly packed)
¼ cup BUTTER
1 qt. day-old BREAD CUBES
¼ cup granulated SUGAR
¼ teaspoon CINNAMON

Combine nectarines and brown sugar in 1 1/2 quart baking dish. Melt butter in large saucepan; mix in bread cubes, granulated sugar and cinnamon til coated. Spread over fruit; bake in preheated 350 F oven 25 minutes or til heated through. (Makes 6 servings)

WALNUT NECTARINE CHUTNEY

3 or 4 fresh Calif. NECTARINES
1/3 cup WALNUTS
¾ cup dried CURRANTS
¼ cup ONION
½ teaspoon GINGER
¼ teaspoon CAYENNE
½ teaspoon SALT
1½ cups CIDER VINEGAR
1 cup BROWN SUGAR (firmly packed)

Chop nectarines to measure two cups. Put walnuts, currants, and onion through food chopper (using fine blade). Combine in saucepan with nectarines and all remaining ingredients. Bring to boil; simmer one hour (or til dark brown in color).

GINGER BASTED CHICKEN 'n NECTARINES

Brush chicken pieces or broiler halves with blended melted butter, honey and ginger. Charcoal broil til tender, turning several times. During last 10 minutes of cooking, broil halves of fresh nectarines, brushed with the butter baste, til lightly browned and serve with broiled chicken.

PLUM-NECTARINE CRUMB PIE

2 cups PLUMS (peeled and quartered)
3 cups NECTARINES (peeled and sliced)
1¼ cups SUGAR
½ cup plus 3 tablespoons FLOUR
½ teaspoon SALT
¼ teaspoon CINNAMON
1/3 cup BUTTER
Unbaked PASTRY for 9 inch pie

Roll out pastry and line 9-inch pie plate. Make a high rim and flute edge. In a large bowl, mix together plums, nectarines, 3/4 cup sugar, 3 tablespoons flour and 1/4 teaspoon salt. Pour fruit mixture into unbaked pastry shell. Combine remaining flour, sugar, salt and add cinnamon. Cut in butter til mixture resembles coarse cornmeal. Sprinkle over fruit mixture. Bake at 400 F 15 minutes. Reduce heat to 350 F and continue baking 30-40 minutes longer. Serve warm or cold.

BISCUIT TOPPED NECTARINES

4 or 5 fresh Calif. NECTARINES
¼ cup WATER
½ cup BROWN SUGAR (firmly packed)
¼ cup BUTTER
½ teaspoon CINNAMON
1 EGG
3 tablespoons MILK
2 tablespoons granulated SUGAR
½ cup BISCUIT MIX
CINNAMON SUGAR

Dice nectarines to measure 2 cups; turn into medium-size skillet. Stir in water, brown sugar, butter and cinnamon; cover and simmer 15 to 20 minutes til nectarines are tender. Beat egg with milk and granulated sugar. Stir in biscuit mix; spoon over top of hot nectarine mixture. Bake on high rack at 400 F for 15 minutes. Sprinkle with cinnamon-sugar; place under broiler 2 or 3 minutes to melt sugar. Serve piping hot with dairy sour cream. (Makes 4 servings)

NECTARINE 'N NUT DESSERT

3 cups fresh Calif. NECTARINES (sliced)
1 cup granulated SUGAR
2 tablespoons FLOUR
4 EGGS
¼ teaspoon SALT
1 cup finely chopped WALNUTS
½ teaspoon VANILLA
2 tablespoons POWDERED SUGAR

Arrange nectarines in 1 1/2 quart casserole. Sprinkle with 1/2 cup granulated sugar mixed with flour. Beat eggs until thick; beat in remaining granulated sugar and salt. Add nuts and vanilla. Spoon over nectarines. Bake at 375 F 30 minutes until topping is browned. Sprinkle with powdered sugar. (Serves 4)

NECTARINE BAVARIAN

3 or 4 fresh Calif. NECTARINES
¼ cup WATER
3 tablespoons LEMON JUICE
¼ cup LIGHT RUM (or orange juice)
1 envelope PLAIN GELATIN
2 EGG WHITES
1 cup WHIPPING CREAM
1 cup POWDERED SUGAR (sifted)
½ teaspoon SALT

Dice nectarines to measure 2 cups. Soften gelatin in water; dissolve over hot water. Remove from heat; add lemon and rum. Stir nectarines into gelatin mix. Whip egg whites until soft peaks form. Whip cream with sugar and salt until stiff. Fold together cream, egg whites and gelatin mix. Pour into 1-quart mold; chill several hours. Unmold onto serving plate. Garnish with nectarine slices, if desired. (Makes 4 servings)

EASY PEEL

To peel California nectarines, plums and peaches, submerge fruit in boiling water for about 30 seconds. Remove with a slotted spoon and dip in cold water. Skins will slip right off.

Apricots

TANGY APRICOT STEW

2 tablespoons SALAD OIL
2 lbs. BEEF STEW MEAT (1½ inch chunks)
2 medium ONIONS (quartered)
1 teaspoon SALT
6 whole ALLSPICE
1 BAY LEAF
1/8 teaspoon PEPPER
1 BEEF BOUILLON CUBE
WATER
3 CARROTS (cut in strips)
1 lb. ZUCCHINI (thinly sliced)
1 cup dried Calif. APRICOTS
½ teaspoon SUGAR
1 teaspoon all-purpose FLOUR

In Dutch oven or large saucepan, heat oil; add beef and brown well on all sides. Add onions, seasonings, bouillon cube, and 2 1/2 cups water. Bring to boil. Reduce heat, cover and simmer an hour (or til meat is tender). Add carrots to beef and cook 5 minutes. Then add zucchini, apricots and sugar; continue cooking 10 more minutes (or til vegetables are tender). Remove bay leaf and discard. Blend flour and 1/4 cup water until smooth. Gradually stir into stew liquid. Cook, stirring constantly, until sauce thickens and boils a minute. Add salt and pepper to taste.

APRICOT HAM GLAZE

1 canned HAM (3 lbs.)
½ cup firmly packed LIGHT BROWN SUGAR
2 teaspoons CORNSTARCH
¼ cup WATER
¼ cup ORANGE MARMALADE
2 teaspoons BUTTER
1 lb. fresh Calif. APRICOTS (pitted and sliced)
¼ cup dark SEEDLESS RAISINS

Place ham in shallow baking pan; bake in 350 F oven 15 minutes. Blend sugar, cornstarch and water in saucepan. Add marmalade and butter. Cook, stirring constantly, til sauce boils. Brush some of the sauce over ham and bake 30 minutes longer. Add apricots and raisins to remaining sauce. Cook over low heat 5 minutes or until apricots are soft.

CRUNCHY APRICOT BARS

1½ cups (11 oz.) dried APRICOTS
4 EGGS
1 cup SUGAR
1 cup firmly packed Light BROWN SUGAR
½ teaspoon SALT
¼ teaspoon ground CARDAMON
1 teaspoon grated LEMON PEEL
¼ cup melted BUTTER
2 cups unsifted all-purpose FLOUR
2 teaspoons BAKING POWDER
1 cup chopped toasted ALMONDS
CONFECTIONERS SUGAR

Soak apricots in hot water one minute and drain. Chop finely and set aside. Beat eggs with sugars, salt, cardamon and lemon peel until very light and fluffy. Stir in butter. Blend in flour and baking powder. Mix in apricots and almonds. Pour batter into greased 9 x 13 baking pan. Bake in 350 F oven 35 minutes (or til cake tests done). Cool 10 minutes in pan, then remove to cooling rack. Sprinkle with confectioners sugar and cut into 36 bars when thoroughly cooled.

BERRY-COT DEEP DISH PIE

1 can (30 oz.) APRICOT HALVES (drained)
1 pkg. (10 oz.) frozen sliced STRAWBERRIES (thawed)
1 tablespoon quick-cooking TAPIOCA
½ cup SUGAR
1 tablespoon BUTTER
Single crust PIE PASTRY
Light CREAM

Combine fruits, tapioca and sugar in 1 1/2 quart baking dish; dot with butter. Roll out pie pastry 1-inch larger than dish; place pastry over fruit. Trim and flute edge of pastry. Brush cream over center of pastry; slash with knife. Bake in 400 F oven 20 to 25 minutes, til crust is lightly browned. Serve warm.

NUTTY APRICOT LOAVES

1½ cups sifted all-purpose FLOUR
2 teaspoons BAKING POWDER
½ teaspoon SALT
¼ teaspoon BAKING SODA
½ cup SUGAR
½ cup chopped dried APRICOTS
½ cup chopped WALNUTS
1 tablespoon grated ORANGE PEEL
1 EGG
¾ cup MILK
¼ cup SALAD OIL

Sift together flour, baking powder, salt and soda into bowl. Mix in sugar, apricots and nuts. Add orange peel, egg, milk and oil. Stir until blended. Pour into greased 8 1/2 x 4 1/2 loaf pan. Bake in 350 F oven 45 minutes or til bread tests done. Cool 10 minutes; remove from pan and cool on rack.

APRICOT WALNUT MUFFINS

1½ cups sifted all-purpose FLOUR
2 teaspoons BAKING POWDER
½ teaspoon SALT
½ teaspoon CINNAMON
½ cup SUGAR
½ cup finely chopped dried Calif. APRICOTS
½ cup finely chopped WALNUTS
1 EGG (slightly beaten)
1 cup MILK
¼ cup SALAD OIL

Sift together flour, baking powder, salt, cinnamon and sugar into bowl. Mix in apricots and walnuts. Combine remaining ingredients and add to dry mixture in bowl. Stir just til ingredients are mixed. Spoon into 12 greased 2 3/4 inch muffin cups (or 42 greased 1 1/2 inch muffin cups). Fill each cup two-thirds full. Bake in 425 F oven until muffins test done--about 25 minutes for larger size, and 15 minutes for smaller.

SPICED APRICOTS

1 can (30 oz.) whole APRICOTS
¼ cup HONEY
2 tablespoons VINEGAR
1 CINNAMON STICK
3 whole CLOVES

Drain apricots, reserving 1/2 cup syrup. Combine honey, vinegar and spices with reserved syrup in saucepan. Bring to a boil and pour over apricots in bowl. Chill several hours.

APRICOT-ORANGE CONSERVE

2 cans (30 oz. each) APRICOT HALVES (drained)
Peel of ½ ORANGE (shredded or finely chopped)
1½ cups ORANGE JUICE
2 tablespoons LEMON JUICE
3½ cups SUGAR
¾ cup chopped WALNUTS

Place all ingredients except nuts in large heavy saucepan; bring mixture to a boil. Simmer, stirring frequently til thickened, about 15 minutes. Stir in nuts. Ladle into four sterilized 8-ounce jelly jars; seal with paraffin. Serve at room temperature as a condiment for meat or poultry, or as a dessert topping.

APRICOT NUTBREAD

1 cup finely chopped, dried Calif. APRICOTS
2 cups warm WATER
2 cups all-purpose FLOUR (unsifted)
1 cup SUGAR
2 teaspoons DOUBLE-ACTING BAKING POWDER
1 teaspoon SALT
¼ teaspoon BAKING SODA
2 tablespoons BUTTER
1 EGG (beaten)
½ cup ORANGE JUICE
½ cup chopped WALNUTS
½ cup CONFECTIONERS SUGAR
2 tablespoons MILK

Soak apricots in warm water for 15 minutes. Drain, reserving 1/4 cup liquid. In a large bowl, combine flour, sugar, baking powder, salt and baking soda. Cut in butter til mixture resembles coarse crumbs. Combine egg, reserved apricot liquid and orange juice; add this mixture plus drained apricots and nuts to flour mixture. Stir just enough to moisten dry ingredients. (Mixture will be lumpy.) Spread in a greased 9x5 loaf pan. Bake in a 350 F oven for 55 minutes (or til done). Cool in pan 10 minutes; remove from pan and cool on wire rack. Combine confectioners' sugar with milk til smooth; spread on top of loaf.

APRICOT PIE

¾ cup SUGAR
¼ teaspoon NUTMEG
¼ teaspoon SALT
1 tablespoon FLOUR
1 tablespoon LEMON JUICE
5 cups fresh APRICOTS (halved)
Two-crust (9") unbaked PIE SHELLS
1 tablespoon BUTTER

Topping

1 tablespoon BUTTER
3 tablespoons FLOUR
1 tablespoon SUGAR
¼ teaspoon SALT

Combine sugar, nutmeg, salt and flour. Sprinkle lemon juice over apricots. Arrange apricots and dry mixture in alternate layers in an UNBAKED pie shell. Dot with butter. Cover with top crust of unbaked pastry.

Crumble topping ingredients and sprinkle over top. Bake at 425 F for 10 minutes; reduce heat to 350 degrees and bake for 25 minutes.

TAHOE BEEF BALLS

1½ lbs. GROUND BEEF
1 cup WHEAT GERM
½ cups roasted ALMONDS
1 cup CHICKEN BOUILLON (or dry white wine)
½ of 1 can condensed ONION SOUP (undiluted)
1½ teaspoons SALT
¼ teaspoon PEPPER
1 can CREAM OF MUSHROOM SOUP (undiluted)
2 tablespoons MARGARINE
½ can ONION SOUP
½ cup WINE

Mix ground beef, wheat germ, almonds, bouillon, undiluted onion soup, salt and pepper together into 24 balls. Combine mushroom soup (undiluted), margarine, remaining onion soup, and 1/2 cup wine in skillet. Heat to boiling, then add beef balls, and simmer uncovered, turning occasionally til done. Serve over hot cooked noodles or rice. Sprinkle with almonds.

GOLD CAMP RABBIT

1 RABBIT (or 1 Frying Chicken)
½ cup FLOUR
1 teaspoon SALT
1 teaspoon DRY MUSTARD
½ teaspoon each: THYME and ROSEMARY
¼ teaspoon PEPPER
3 tablespoons MARGARINE
½ cup DRY VERMOUTH (or Chicken Broth)
1 cup YOGURT
1 tablespoon PARSLEY

Cut rabbit (or chicken) into serving pieces and shake in bag with flour and spices. Heat margarine in skillet and brown rabbit pieces (turning once). Add vermouth (or chicken broth). Cover and simmer 15 minutes (or til fork-tender). Transfer rabbit to warm platter. To pan drippings, add yogurt and parsley. Salt to taste. Spoon sauce over rabbit and sprinkle with toasted sliced almonds. (Serves 4)

ALMOND BURGERS

1 lb. GROUND BEEF
¼ cup WHEAT GERM
1 EGG
1 teaspoon GARLIC SALT
¼ teaspoon PEPPER
4 English MUFFINS
½ cup GRAPE JELLY
½ cup CATSUP
3 tablespoons toasted ALMONDS

Mix ground beef with wheat germ, egg, salt and pepper. Shape into four burgers. Grill over hot coals, turning once. Meanwhile toast English muffins. Melt grape jelly, blend in catsup and add almonds. Place each burger on a muffin half, topped with sauce. Cover with muffin half and serve with relishes.

CHOCOLATE-ALMOND ZUCCHINI BREAD

3 EGGS
2 cups SUGAR
1 cup SALAD OIL
2 oz. unsweetened CHOCOLATE
1 teaspoon VANILLA
2 cups grated ZUCCHINI
3 cups FLOUR
1 teaspoon SALT
1 teaspoon CINNAMON
¼ teaspoon BAKING POWDER
1 teaspoon SODA
1 cup ALMONDS (chopped)

Beat eggs til lemon-colored. Beat in sugar and oil. Melt chocolate over hot water and stir into egg mixture along with vanilla and zucchini. Sift flour with salt, cinnamon, baking powder and soda. Stir into zucchini mixture with almonds. Mix well. Bake in 2 well-oiled 9x5 loaf pans at 350 F for one hour and 20 minutes (or til done). Cool in pans 15 to 20 minutes and turn onto rack. Cool thoroughly before serving. (Makes 2 loaves)

ALMOND OATIES

¾ cup all purpose FLOUR
½ cup whole wheat FLOUR
1 teaspoon BAKING SODA
1 teaspoon SALT
1 cup SUGAR
1 cup BROWN SUGAR
1 cup BUTTER
2 EGGS
1 teaspoon VANILLA
1½ cups sliced ALMONDS
3 cups quick-cooking OATS

Mix all-purpose flour (unsifted) with whole wheat flour, baking soda and salt. Cream sugars with butter, eggs, and vanilla until fluffy. Blend in flour mixture. Stir in almonds and oats. Divide dough into halves; shape each half into a 10 x 1 1/2 inch roll on plastic and wrap separately. Chill til firm. Slice thin. Bake on greased baking sheet at 350 F for 10 minutes. (Dough may be kept a week in refrigerator). Recipe makes about 60 cookies.

ALMOND CHOCOS

2 oz. unsweetened CHOCOLATE
1 can (14 oz.) condensed MILK
2 cups Graham Cracker CRUMBS
½ teaspoon CINNAMON
½ teaspoon SALT
½ cup roasted, diced ALMONDS
3 doz. whole, blanched ALMONDS

Melt chocolate in top of double boiler. Stir in condensed milk, crumbs, cinnamon, salt and almonds. Drop by spoonfuls onto greased baking sheet; flatten with metal spatula. Press a whole almond into each. Bake at 325 F for 15 minutes and remove from pan immediately. (Makes about 3 dozen cookies)

Roasted Almonds (Diced)

Chop whole natural (unblanched) almonds and pour them into a shallow pan which has been lightly coated with oil or butter (and salt, if desired). Heat in a 300 F oven for about 15 minutes, stirring frequently.

BEAN SPROUT ALMOND SALAD

1/3 cup toasted ALMONDS
2 cups fresh BEAN SPROUTS (or drained canned)
½ cups sliced CELERY
2 tablespoons chopped GREEN PEPPER
¼ cup MAYONNAISE
1 tablespoon LEMON JUICE
1/8 teaspoon ground GINGER
¼ teaspoon PAPRIKA
1 teaspoon SUGAR

Toss almonds with bean sprouts, celery, green pepper. Blend remaining ingredients and combine with almond mixture. Spoon over platter of torn salad greens.

ALMOND FISH SAUCE

½ cup BUTTER
1/3 cup toasted sliced ALMONDS
½ teaspoon SALT
3 tablespoons LEMON JUICE (fresh)

Melt butter, add almonds and stir over medium heat until almonds are golden. Stir in salt and fresh lemon (or orange) juice and serve over cooked fish.

ALMOND-SAUCED OMELET

¼ cup PARSLEY sprigs
1 canned seeded GREEN CHILI
1 GREEN ONION (chopped)
¼ teaspoon SALT
½ cup SOUR CREAM
1/3 cup roasted ALMONDS

In blender, puree parsley sprigs (packed) with green chili, chopped onion, salt and sour cream. Turn into saucepan. Stir in almonds. Heat thoroughly (but do not boil).

3 EGGS
2 tablespoons WATER
¼ teaspoon THYME
3 oz. CREAM CHEESE
2 tablespoons BUTTER

Beat eggs with water and thyme. Cube cream cheese and stir into egg mixture. Heat butter in skillet til bubbly; pour in egg mixture. Lift omelet edges and tilt omelet pan so uncooked portion flows to bottom of frypan and cooks. Slide omelet onto heated platter and fold. Pour almond sauce over omelet.

ALMOND GRANOLA

1½ cups slivered ALMONDS
4 cups long-cooking OATS
½ cup shredded COCONUT
1 cup toasted WHEAT GERM
½ cup VEGETABLE OIL
½ cup HONEY

Mix almonds, oats, coconut and wheat germ. Combine oil and honey and work liquid into oat mixture (using fingers to remove lumps). Turn into large, shallow pan. Bake 30 minutes at 350 F stirring every 10 minutes for even browning. Cool, stirring occasionally, to break up any lumps. Store in airtight containers in freezer. (Makes two pounds)

ALMOND FUDGE

8 oz. semi-sweet CHOCOLATE
½ cup superfine SUGAR
1 cup roasted ALMONDS (diced)
1 EGG (slightly beaten)

Melt chocolate over hot water. Add sugar, almonds and egg. Mix thoroughly. Turn out onto a bed of powdered sugar on a piece of foil or plastic wrap. Pull up sides of foil to help coat mixture with powdered sugar and shape like a sausage (1 1/2 to 2 inches in diameter, about 12 inches long). Chill thoroughly. To serve, cut thin slices. (Makes 48 slices)

KUNG FU CLUSTERS

3 chocolate ALMOND BARS
1 can (3 oz.) CHOW MEIN NOODLES
2 tablespoons slivered ALMONDS

Melt almond bars in top of double boiler. Stir in chow mein noodles and slivered almonds (toasted and chopped). Form into clusters on wax paper. Chill. Garnish with bits of candied ginger.

To Blanch and Sliver Almonds

Heat water to boiling and pour over shelled almonds. Let almonds set half an hour in water. Drain and slip skins off. Cut nuts lengthwise into several strips. To brown slivers, place in baking pan in oven, or brown lightly in butter.

ALMOND BALLS

1 pkg. (8 oz.) CREAM CHEESE
½ cup roasted, diced ALMONDS
6 oz. semi-sweet CHOCOLATE CHIPS
1/3 cup candied CHERRIES

Mix cream cheese (softened) with almonds, chocolate chips and candied cherries (chopped and drained). Shape into small balls. Chill. (Makes about two dozen).

ALMOND HIKING BARS

½ cup BUTTER
½ cup BROWN SUGAR
½ cup quick-cooking OATS
½ cup Whole Wheat FLOUR (unsifted)
½ cup all-purpose FLOUR (unsifted)
½ cup WHEAT GERM
2 teaspoons grated ORANGE RIND
2 EGGS
1 cup whole blanched ALMONDS
¼ cup RAISINS
¼ cup flaked COCONUT
½ cup semi-sweet CHOCOLATE BITS

Cream butter with 1/4 cup brown sugar til soft; beat in oats, flours, wheat germ and orange rind. Pat into 8-inch square pan. Mix eggs, almonds, raisins, coconut, chocolate bits and 1/4 cup brown sugar (packed). Pour over base and spread out evenly. Bake at 350 F for 35 minutes (or til almonds are golden brown.) Cool and cut into a dozen bars. Wrap in aluminum foil.

Walnuts

OLD FASHIONED NUT BREAD

1½ cups Diamond WALNUTS
3 cups sifted all-purpose FLOUR
1 cup granulated SUGAR
4 teaspoons BAKING POWDER
1½ teaspoons SALT
1 EGG (lightly beaten)
¼ cup SHORTENING (melted)
1½ cups MILK
1 teaspoon VANILLA

Coarsely chop walnuts. Resift flour with sugar, baking powder and salt. Add egg, shortening, milk and vanilla to dry mixture. Stir just until all of flour is moistened. Stir in walnuts. Turn into greased 9x5x3 loaf pan, or divide batter between 2 greased #2 1/2 cans. Bake at 350 F about 1 hour 20 minutes (for loaf), or 1 hour 10 minutes (for round loaves).

Streusel Variation

1/3 cup BROWN SUGAR (packed)
1½ tablespoons FLOUR
1 teaspoon CINNAMON
2 tablespoons BUTTER

Blend sugar, flour, cinnamon and butter together in a small mixing bowl. Prepare the batter for Old Fashioned Diamond Nut Bread. Turn half of batter into loaf pan. Sprinkle streusel mixture over batter and top with remaining batter. Bake as directed.

DIAMOND WHITE FUDGE

2 cups granulated SUGAR
½ cup SOUR CREAM
1/3 cup white CORN SYRUP
2 tablespoons BUTTER
¼ teaspoon SALT
2 teaspoons VANILLA (or rum or brandy flavoring)
¼ cup quartered candied CHERRIES
1 cup coarsely-chopped Diamond WALNUTS

Combine first five ingredients in saucepan; bring to a boil slowly, stirring til sugar dissolves. Boil, without stirring, over medium heat, to 236 F on candy thermometer (or til a little mixture dropped in cold water forms a soft ball). Remove from heat and let stand 15 minutes. DO NOT STIR. Add flavoring; beat til mixture starts to lose its gloss (about 8 minutes). Stir in the candied cherries and walnuts and quickly pour into a greased shallow pan (or into a foil-lined pan). Cool and cut.

SPICY-SUGARED WALNUTS

1 cup granulated SUGAR
1 teaspoon SALT
2 teaspoons CINNAMON
½ teaspoon NUTMEG
½ teaspoon CLOVES
½ cup WATER
2 cups Calif. WALNUT HALVES

In a saucepan combine sugar, salt, cinnamon, nutmeg, cloves, and water. Bring to a boil. Boil, stirring frequently, to 236 F on a candy thermometer. Remove from heat. Add walnuts and stir til creamy. Turn out on waxed paper, and separate walnuts, using two forks.

BROWNIE FRUITCAKE

1½ cups Calif. WALNUTS
1 cup halved candied CHERRIES
1 cup mixed candied FRUITS
1 cup sliced DATES
½ cup hot COFFEE
¼ cup powdered COCOA
1¾ cups sifted all-purpose FLOUR
¾ teaspoon SALT
¼ teaspoon BAKING SODA
¼ teaspoon CINNAMON
1/8 teaspoon CLOVES
½ cup BUTTER
1¼ cups BROWN SUGAR (packed)
2 EGGS
1 teaspoon VANILLA
4 to 6 WALNUT HALVES

Chop walnuts coarsely; combine with candied fruits and dates. Stir coffee into cocoa and set aside to cool. Line a loaf pan (11 x 3 1/2 x 2 3/4) with one thickness of greased brown paper and one of greased waxed paper, allowing to extend about an inch above sides and ends of pan. Resift flour with salt, baking soda and spices. Cream butter and brown sugar together well. Beat in eggs and vanilla (mixture will appear curdled). Blend in flour mixture alternately with cocoa mixture. Stir in walnuts and fruits. Turn into prepared pan. Arrange walnut halves on top. Place a shallow pan of hot water on floor of oven. Bake cake on lowest rack at 300 F with a single sheet of brown paper resting over paper lining the pan, for 2 to 2 1/4 hours (til cake tests done). Cool in pan. Makes one 3-pound cake .

To decorate: arrange halves of candied cherries and strips of citron or candied pineapple between walnut halves.

DOUBLE WALNUT FRUITCAKE

2½ cups Calif. WALNUTS
1 cup candied PINEAPPLE CHUNKS
1 cup halved CANDIED CHERRIES
1 cup sliced DATES
½ cup golden RAISINS
1½ cups sifted all-purpose FLOUR
1 teaspoon BAKING POWDER
1 teaspoon SALT
2/3 cup BUTTER
1 cup BROWN SUGAR (packed)
3 EGGS
1 teaspoon VANILLA

Chop one cup walnuts coarsely; combine with candied fruits, dates and raisins. Grate remaining 1 1/2 cups walnuts with Mouli grater (or put in blender, about 1/4 cup at a time, and blend to a fine meal). Resift flour with baking powder and salt. Cream butter and brown sugar together well. Beat in eggs, one at a time (Mixture will look curdled). Blend in vanilla, then flour mixture and grated walnuts. Fold in walnut-fruit mixture. Turn into a well-greased 12 x 4 1/4 x 3 loaf pan, or other pan with 2-quart capacity. Place a shallow pan of hot water on floor of oven. Bake cake on lowest rack at 300 F for about 2 hours, til cake tests done. Cool in pan 30 minutes, then turn out onto wire rack to finish cooling. (Makes one 3 1/4 pound loaf)

To decorate: mix powdered sugar with water to thin pouring consistency. Drizzle over top of cake. Pile mixed candied fruits and peels on top of cake down the center.

WHITE WALNUT FRUITCAKE

1½ cups Calit. WALNUTS
1½ cups halved candied CHERRIES
Diced, candied fruits:
- 1 cup PINEAPPLE
- ¾ cup ORANGE PEEL
- ¾ cup LEMON PEEL

¾ cup diced CITRON
¾ cup BRANDY
2 cups sifted all-purpose FLOUR
1 teaspoon SALT
1 teaspoon MACE
¾ teaspoon BAKING POWDER
¾ cup BUTTER
1 cup granulated SUGAR
4 EGGS (separated)
1 tablespoon grated ORANGE PEEL
½ teaspoon CREAM OF TARTAR

Chop walnuts coarsely and set aside. Combine candied fruits and peels. Pour 1/2 cup brandy over fruits, stir to moisten, cover and let stand for several hours or overnight. Line a 9-inch tube pan with one thickness of greased brown paper and one of greased waxed paper. Resift flour with salt, mace and baking powder. Cream butter with sugar until light and fluffy. Beat in egg yolks. Add grated orange peel, then sifted dry ingredients alternately with remaining 1/4 cup brandy. Fold in walnuts, candied fruits and any brandy remaining on them. Beat egg whites with cream of tartar just until stiff. Fold gently into the fruit mixture. Spoon into prepared pan and spread level. Place a shallow pan of hot water on floor of oven. Bake on lowest rack at 300 F for about 2 1/2 hours (til cake tests done). Cool in pan. Makes one 4-pound cake).

To decorate: sift powdered sugar lightly over top of cake. Decorate with strips of citron and candied cherries.

BANANA WALNUT FRUITCAKE

1½ cups Calif. WALNUTS
2 cups mixed CANDIED FRUITS
1¾ cups sifted all-purpose FLOUR
1 teaspoon BAKING POWDER
1 teaspoon SALT
¼ teaspoon BAKING SODA
¼ teaspoon NUTMEG
2/3 cup BUTTER
¾ cup granulated SUGAR
2 large EGGS
1 cup mashed BANANAS

Chop walnuts coarsely. Chop candied fruits fine and combine with walnuts; set aside. Resift flour with baking powder, salt, baking soda and nutmeg. Cream butter with sugar til fluffy. Beat in eggs, one at a time. Blend in flour mixture alternately with mashed banana at low speed on mixer (or by hand). Pour batter over fruit-walnut mixture and blend well. Turn into a well-greased tube pan (about 2 quart capacity). Bake cake on lowest rack at 300 F for 1 1/4 hours (or until pick inserted in center comes out clean and dry). Let stand 15 minutes in pan, then invert onto wire rack to cool. Serve plain or with a light sifting of powdered sugar over top. (Makes one 3-lb. cake)

WALNUT PIE

½ cup BROWN SUGAR (packed)
2 tablespoons all-purpose FLOUR
1¼ cups light CORN SYRUP
3 tablespoons BUTTER
¼ teaspoon SALT
3 EGGS
1½ teaspoons VANILLA
1 cup halves and pieces Diamond WALNUTS

Mix brown sugar and flour in saucepan. Add corn syrup, butter and salt, and warm over low heat just until butter is melted. In large bowl, beat eggs with vanilla. Stir in sugar mixture. Turn into pie shell and sprinkle with walnuts. Bake on lower rack at 350 F for 40 to 45 minutes (til filling is set in center). Cool before cutting.

9" Pie Shell

1½ cups sifted all-purpose FLOUR
½ teaspoon SALT
½ cup SHORTENING
4 tablespoons COLD MILK (or water)

Resift flour with salt into mixing bowl. Cut in shortening with pastry blender (or 2 knives) til size of peas. Sprinkle milk or water, tablespoon at a time, over dry ingredients, and gently toss with a fork. Mix lightly til all flour is moistened. (If necessary, add 1 or 2 teaspoons extra liquid.) Gather dough together and gently shape into ball. Roll out on floured cloth covered board to 10-inch circle. Roll from center to outside evenly in all directions. Lift rolling pin at edge of dough to keep edges from becoming too thin. Fold dough in half and lift into pie pan. Unfold and ease dough gently into place to fit pan. Build up a shallow fluted edge on pie rim.

WALNUT BROWNIES

2 EGGS
1 cup SUGAR
½ teaspoon SALT
1 teaspoon VANILLA
1/3 cup SHORTENING (melted)
2 squares (1 oz. each) UNSWEETENED CHOCOLATE (melted)
¾ cup sifted all-purpose FLOUR
1 cup chopped Diamond WALNUTS

Beat eggs lightly with spoon. Stir in sugar, salt and vanilla, then melted shortening and chocolate. Stir in flour and walnuts together. DO NOT BEAT AT ANY TIME. Spread mixture in an 8 or 9-inch greased square pan and bake at 325 F for 30 minutes. (Brownies should still be soft). Let cool in pan. Cut into small bars.

WALNUT SALAD CROUTONS

Saute walnut kernels in butter over moderately low heat til golden brown. Season to taste with salt, onion or garlic salt, or seasoned salt while still warm. Cool and add to salads.

Pecans

CRUNCHY TOP COFFEECAKE

2 cups sifted, all-purpose FLOUR
1 cup SUGAR
1 tablespoon BAKING POWDER
1 teaspoon SALT
1 cup MILK
1/3 cup soft BUTTER
1 EGG
½ cup finely cut Funsten WALNUTS
¼ cup SUGAR
1 teaspoon CINNAMON

Sift flour, sugar, baking powder and salt into 3-quart bowl of electric mixer. Beat in milk, butter and egg at medium speed (2 minutes), scraping sides of bowl often. Pour into greased and floured 9-inch square pan. Combine walnuts, sugar and cinnamon in bowl. Mix thoroughly and sprinkle over batter. Bake in 350 F oven about 35 minutes (or til cake pulls away from sides of pan). Serve warm.

PECAN-OATMEAL COOKIES

¾ cup sifted, all-purpose FLOUR
½ teaspoon SALT
½ teaspoon CINNAMON
¼ teaspoon BAKING SODA
1 cup uncooked quick rolled OATS
1/3 cup SUGAR
1/3 cup firmly packed BROWN SUGAR
½ cup soft BUTTER
1 EGG
1 teaspoon VANILLA
1 cup cut-up Funsten PECANS
½ cup RAISINS

Sift flour, salt, cinnamon and baking soda onto waxed paper. Mix oats into dry ingredients. Beat sugar, brown sugar, butter, egg and vanilla in 1 1/2 quart bowl til fluffy. Mix in dry ingredients. Stir in pecans and raisins. Drop with 2 teaspoons onto greased cooky sheet. Bake in center of 375 F oven for 10 to 12 minutes. (Makes about 3 dozen cookies)

GOLDEN PECAN PIE

3 EGGS
1 cup dark CORN SYRUP
1 cup SUGAR
2 tablespoons BUTTER (melted)
1 cup PECANS (whole)
1/8 teaspoon SALT
1 teaspoon VANILLA
Unbaked 9" PIE SHELL

Mix corn syrup, sugar, and butter with eggs. Add pecans, salt and vanilla and stir to blend. Pour into unbaked pie shell. Bake in 400 F oven 15 minutes; reduce heat to 350 F and bake another 25 to 30 minutes. (Filling will be slightly less set in center than around edge.)

Roasted Nuts

Set oven at 300 F. Pour nuts into shallow pan. Roast, stirring often, about 15 to 20 minutes, or til golden brown.

Strawberries

BAKED CUSTARD with STRAWBERRY SAUCE

4 large EGGS
1/3 cup SUGAR
¼ teaspoon SALT
3 cups MILK
1 teaspoon VANILLA EXTRACT
Sweetened sliced STRAWBERRIES

Beat eggs slightly and stir in sugar and salt. Scald milk and gradually stir into egg mixture. Add vanilla and pour into six 6-ounce custard cups (or a 1/2-quart glass casserole). Set in shallow pan and add 3/4" hot water. Bake in preheated 325 F oven 45 minutes for small custards (or 1 1/4 hours for casserole), or til small spatula comes out clean when inserted in center of custard. Remove from hot water, cool, then chill. Unmold small custards (and large one, if desired). Serve with fresh berries.

STRAWBERRY SHORTCAKE LAYERS

3 cups FLOUR
3¼ teaspoons double-acting
  BAKING POWDER
3 tablespoons SUGAR
1¼ teaspoons SALT
½ cup soft SHORTENING
1 EGG (well beaten)
2/3 cup MILK (about)
3 pints STRAWBERRIES
Heavy CREAM

Mix flour, baking powder, sugar and salt in bowl. Cut in shortening. Add egg and enough milk to make a soft dough, mixing with a fork. Knead lightly about 20 turns on a floured board. Divide in thirds. Pat out each third in greased 9" round layer-cake pan. Bake in preheated 450 F oven about 15 minutes. Wash and hull berries. Cut in halves and sweeten to taste. Cool shortcake layers and put together with fresh berries between layers and on top. Serve with cream.

STRAWBERRY LEMON PUDDING

¼ cup BUTTER
2 EGGS (separated)
3 tablespoons LEMON JUICE
1 pkg. (10 oz.) frozen sliced
  Calif. STRAWBERRIES (thawed)
1 tablespoon grated
  LEMON RIND
Dash SALT
¼ cup SUGAR
2 cups diced SPONGE CAKE
½ cup chopped WALNUTS

Melt butter; add egg yolks, lemon juice, undrained strawberries, lemon rind and salt. Cook over low heat, stirring constantly til slightly thickened. Beat egg whites til foamy. Gradually add sugar, one tablespoon at a time, beating constantly until stiff and glossy. Fold egg white mixture, diced cake and walnuts into strawberry mixture. Turn into lightly buttered 1 1/2 quart baking dish. Bake at 350 F for 45 minutes (or til knife inserted in center comes out clean). Makes 6 servings.

STRAWBERRY SHORTCAKE ROUNDS

½ cup BUTTER (softened)
¼ cup SUGAR
1¼ cups all-purpose FLOUR
1 qt. vanilla ICE CREAM
2 pkgs. (1 lb. each) frozen sliced STRAWBERRIES

Mix butter and sugar with pastry blender or fork. Add flour and mix til crumbly. Then, with hands, mix gently until dough is formed. Roll 1/4'' thick on lightly floured board and cut in 16 rounds with 2 1/2'' cookie cutter. Put on baking sheet and prick several times with fork. Bake in preheated 325 F oven 20 minutes, or til lightly browned. Cool. To serve, put ice cream and berries between and on top of rounds.

PLUM and STRAWBERRY PIE

1 cup STRAWBERRIES (crushed)
¼ cup CURRANT JELLY
1 tablespoon CORNSTARCH
1 pkg. (8 oz.) CREAM CHEESE (softened)
1/3 cup SUGAR
Juice and grated rind of ½ ORANGE
1 8-inch baked PIE SHELL
1½ cups fresh Calif. PLUMS (sliced)

In saucepan, combine strawberries, currant jelly and cornstarch. Cook over low heat, stirring constantly, til sauce thickens. In a bowl, whip cream cheese with sugar, orange peel and juice. Spread in cooled pie shell. Arrange plum slices on cream cheese mixture. Pour strawberry glaze over top. Chill. Serve with sour cream or whipped cream. (Makes 6 servings)

STRAWBERRIES AMBROSIA

1 pkg. (10 oz.) frozen sliced Calif. STRAWBERRIES (thawed)
¼ lb. (16) MARSHMALLOWS (quartered)
1 teaspoon grated LEMON PEEL
2 tablespoons LEMON JUICE
1 medium ORANGE (pared and diced)
Dash SALT
1 cup flaked COCONUT
½ cup heavy CREAM (whipped)

Combine strawberries, marshmallows, lemon peel, lemon juice, orange and salt; toss lightly. Chill 1 hour. Fold in coconut and cream. (Makes 4 servings)

FRESH STRAWBERRY PIE

1 baked 9-inch PIE SHELL
2 pint boxes STRAWBERRIES
1 cup SUGAR
3 tablespoons CORNSTARCH
½ cup WATER
1 tablespoon fresh LEMON JUICE
1 cup WHIPPING CREAM
¼ cup SUGAR
½ teaspoon VANILLA

Wash berries thoroughly and remove stems. Mash 2 cups of berries (reserve few for garnish). Slice remaining berries and arrange in bottom of baked pie shell. Sprinkle lightly with two tablespoons sugar. Blend sugar and cornstarch in a saucepan. Add water, lemon juice and mashed strawberries. Cook over medium heat til thickened, stirring constantly. Pour glaze over berries in pie shell. Chill. Top with whipped cream to which sugar and vanilla have been added. Garnish with berries.

OLD-FASHIONED STRAWBERRY SHORTCAKE

2 cups all purpose FLOUR
¼ cup SUGAR
3 teaspoons BAKING POWDER
½ teaspoon SALT
½ cup BUTTER
¾ cup MILK

Preheat oven to 450 F. Sift flour with sugar, baking powder, and salt. Cut butter into chunks and add to flour mixture. Using pastry blender, cut butter into small particles, til coated thoroughly with flour. Make well in center of mixture and add milk. Mix quickly with fork to moisten flour, but do not overmix. (Mixture will be lumpy.) Turn into greased 8x8x2 baking pan. Press out dough to fit corners of pan. Bake in 450 F oven for 12 minutes (or til cake tester comes out clean). Loosen from pan with sharp knife and turn out to cool on wire rack. After berries are prepared, slit cake in half crosswise, using a serrated knife. Put bottom of cake on serving platter, cut side up. Spoon sliced berries over bottom half of cake. Place top of cake over berries, and spoon remaining berries over top. Garnish with whipped cream and strawberries. (Serves 6)

Berry Topping

3 pint boxes STRAWBERRIES
¾ cup SUGAR
1 cup heavy CREAM
2 tablespoons CONFECTIONER'S SUGAR

Wash berries in cold water, drain, remove hulls, and slice berries into a bowl. Add sugar and mix well. Set aside til shortcake is prepared.

To whip cream, beat with rotary beater til stiff, and gradually stir in confectioners sugar.

STRAWBERRY ICECREAM SODA

Put 1/3 cup frozen or crushed sweetened fresh strawberries, 3 tablespoons milk and a large scoop of strawberry ice cream in a large glass. Almost fill the glass with chilled carbonated water, stir, and serve immediately.

FREEZER STRAWBERRY JAM

4 cups hulled, well crushed STRAWBERRIES
1 pkg. (2 oz.) powdered PECTIN
1 cup light CORN SYRUP
5½ cups SUGAR
4 tablespoons LEMON JUICE

Turn crushed strawberries into 2-quart pot. Stir vigorously, sifting in powdered pectin slowly. Let stand 20 minutes, stirring strawberries occasionally to dissolve pectin. Pour in corn syrup and mix well. Gradually stir in sugar. When sugar is completely dissolved, stir in lemon juice. Ladle jam into jars, cover and place in freezer for 24 hours. (Jam can be stored in refrigerator after freezing period.)

FRENCH GRAPE PUDDING

3 cups (1 lb.) Calif. seedless GRAPES
2 large APPLES (peeled & diced)
½ cup WALNUTS (chopped)
1½ cups MILK
4 EGGS
2 teaspoons VANILLA
½ cup FLOUR
½ cup SUGAR
Powdered SUGAR and CINNAMON
Sweetened WHIPPED CREAM

Scatter fruit and nuts in buttered 2-quart casserole. Blend milk, eggs and vanilla in blender. Add flour and sugar; blend thoroughly and pour over fruit. Bake in middle of oven for 1 1/2 hours at 350 F. Cool slightly. Dust with powdered sugar and cinnamon. Serve warm with whipped cream.

SPICED FALL GRAPES

4 cups (2 lbs.) Calif. GRAPES
3 cups WHITE VINEGAR
4½ cups SUGAR
2 sticks CINNAMON
1 teaspoon WHOLE CLOVES
½ teaspoon WHOLE ALLSPICE
½ teaspoon ground CORIANDER
¼ teaspoon MACE
3 strips ORANGE PEEL
3 strips LEMON PEEL

Wash grapes and place in a one-quart, sterilized, pickling jar. Bring vinegar and sugar to a boil, stirring until sugar is dissolved. Add spices and peels, simmer five minutes, then remove from heat. Cool slightly. Pour liquid over grapes. Seal jar. (Makes one quart)

FRESH GRAPE CHUTNEY

1 whole LEMON (seeded and sliced)
1½ cups LIGHT BROWN SUGAR (firmly packed)
1½ cups WHITE WINE VINEGAR
1 large ONION (chopped)
2 cloves GARLIC (minced)
1 tablespoon SALT
2 teaspoons GINGER
1 teaspoon CURRY
1 pkg. (4 oz.) slivered ALMONDS
2 large green APPLES (unpeeled and chopped)
1½ lbs. Calif. GRAPES (stemmed)

Into a heavy kettle, put lemon, sugar, vinegar, onion, garlic, salt, ginger and curry. Bring to a boil and continue boiling uncovered, stirring occasionally, for 20 minutes (or til mixture thickens slightly and lemon is tender.) Stir in almonds and apples; cook 3 minutes. Stir in grapes; cook 2 minutes more--just enough to heat grapes through. Pour into hot sterilized jars, to within 1/2 inch of top of jar. Seal with sterilized screw-on lids. Cool. Store in cool place. (Makes 3 pints)

APPLE GRAPE FRUITCAKE

1 cup SUGAR
¼ cup BUTTER
1 teaspoon CINNAMON
¼ teaspoon NUTMEG
1 teaspoon VANILLA
2 cups APPLES (coarsely grated)
1½ cups Calif. GRAPES (halved and seeded)
½ cup chopped WALNUTS
1 cup FLOUR
1 teaspoon BAKING SODA

In mixing bowl, cream together sugar, butter, cinnamon and nutmeg. Stir in vanilla, apples, grapes and nuts. Combine flour and baking soda; sift into creamed mixture, blend well. Spread batter in lightly buttered 8-inch square cake pan. Bake in 350 F oven 45 minutes (or til cake tests done). Glaze warm cake with Lemon Icing.

Lemon Icing

1 tablespoon LEMON RIND (grated)
1 cup sifted powdered SUGAR
¼ cup LEMON JUICE

Mix sugar with grated rind and juice. Beat until smooth.

GRAPE MOSAIC CHEESECAKE

1 cup Graham Cracker CRUMBS
¼ cup melted BUTTER
1½ lbs. CREAM CHEESE
3 EGGS
¾ cup SUGAR
½ teaspoon SALT
1½ teaspoons VANILLA
1 cup Calif. GRAPES (assorted colors, halved & seeded)

Mix graham cracker crumbs with butter; press into 8-inch spring-form pan. Beat cream cheese just until soft; add eggs, one at a time, then sugar and salt. Stir in vanilla; pour into pan. Bake in 350 F oven 1 1/2 hours. Cool. Top with grape halves or whole seedless grapes. Drizzle with Cheese Fondant Glaze.

Cheese Fondant Glaze

1 pkg. (3 oz.) CREAM CHEESE
1 EGG YOLK
1 teaspoon VANILLA
1 cup sifted powdered SUGAR
MILK

Beat cheese until soft. Add egg yolk and vanilla; blend well. Gradually add powdered sugar, beating til smooth. Thin with milk to desired consistency.

PICKLED GRAPES

2 lbs. (about 4 cups) Calif. Thompson seedless GRAPES
1 cup WHITE WINE VINEGAR
2 cups WATER
1 teaspoon SALT
1½ cups SUGAR
2 PEPPERCORNS
1 CLOVE

Pull grapes from stems and wash well. Pour grapes into a 2-quart sterilized jar. Put rest of ingredients into a saucepan and bring to a boil, stirring til sugar is dissolved. Pour over grapes. Let stand at least 3 days before using. (Makes 2 quarts)

CHAMPAGNE WREATH

2 pkg. (6 oz. each) Lemon Flavor GELATIN
2¼ cups boiling WATER
1 bottle (4/5 qt.) chilled CHAMPAGNE (or Ginger Ale)
3 cups Calif. seedless GRAPES
2 cups sliced STRAWBERRIES

Dissolve gelatin in boiling water. Add champagne and chill until partially thickened. Add fruit. Pour into 9 (or 10) cup ring mold and chill until firm. Unmold on serving platter and garnish with salad greens if desired. (Makes 8 servings)

GRAPE CURRY

1 cup Calif. seedless GRAPES
½ cup ONION (chopped)
2 tablespoons BUTTER
¼ cup FLOUR
1 can (13¾ oz.) Chicken BROTH
¼ cup dry white WINE
1 tablespoon CURRY POWDER
1 teaspoon SALT
1 lb. cooked large SHRIMP
1 tablespoon LEMON JUICE
Hot cooked RICE

Puree grapes in blender. Cook onion in butter in large saucepan over low heat til limp. Stir in flour; gradually add broth. Add grape puree, wine, curry powder and salt. Stir over low heat til sauce thickens (about 10 minutes). Add shrimp and lemon juice. Heat thoroughly. Serve over rice with whole grapes.

PLUM and GRAPE RELISH

3 lbs. fresh Calif. PLUMS
3 lbs. seedless GRAPES
3 cups WATER
SUGAR
3 cups WHITE VINEGAR
1 tablespoon CINNAMON
1 tablespoon ALLSPICE
2 tablespoons CLOVES
1½ teaspoons NUTMEG

In large saucepan cook fruit in water til very soft (about 30 minutes). Press through fine sieve. Discard pits and skins. Measure pulp; add HALF that amount of sugar; mix with rest of ingredients in heavy pot. Cook, stirring frequently, til mixture is very thick (about 1 hour 20 minutes). Skim and pour into sterilized jars. Seal tightly. (Makes about four half-pints)

HARVEST GRAPE APPLES

4 baking APPLES
1½ cups Calif. GRAPES (halved and seeded)
2 tablespoons BROWN SUGAR
½ cup WALNUTS (chopped)
1 tablespoon CORN SYRUP
1 tablespoon RUM

Wash and core apples, making a large center hole for grapes. Mix together grapes, sugar, nuts, corn syrup and rum. Fill apple hollows with mixture. Bake in 350 F oven 45 minutes (or til apples are tender.) Serve with Rum Ice Cream Sauce.

Rum Ice Cream Sauce

1 pint VANILLA ICE CREAM
2 tablespoons RUM

Mix ice cream with rum and spoon over apples. Sprinkle with cinnamon.

Raisins

RAISIN GRANOLA

2 cups old fashioned OATS
1 cup shredded COCONUT
½ cup WHEAT GERM
1½ cups chopped WALNUTS (or almonds)
1 teaspoon SALT
1 can (14 oz.) SWEETENED CONDENSED MILK
¼ cup OIL
1½ cups Sun-Maid RAISINS (red box)

Combine oats, coconut, wheat germ, nuts and salt in a large bowl. Stir in condensed milk; add oil and mix thoroughly. Spread mixture on shallow baking pan lined with waxed paper. Bake in 300 F oven, stirring occasionally for an hour (or til golden). Remove from oven and stir in raisins while still warm. Store in a tightly covered container. (Makes 8 cups)

BARS OF IRON

1 cup dark Calif. RAISINS
½ cup golden Calif. RAISINS
1/3 cup BUTTER
½ cup SUGAR
½ cup golden MOLASSES
1 EGG
1¼ cups WHOLE WHEAT FLOUR
¼ cup NONFAT DRY MILK
¼ cup toasted WHEAT GERM
1½ teaspoons BAKING POWDER
½ teaspoon SODA
½ teaspoon SALT
½ teaspoon GINGER
½ cup liquid MILK
1 cup quick cooking rolled OATS
1 cup sliced ALMONDS

Chop raisins. Cream butter, sugar, molasses and egg together. Combine whole wheat flour, nonfat dry milk, wheat germ, baking powder, soda, salt and ginger, and mix lightly. Blend into the creamed mixture alternately with liquid milk. Stir in oats, raisins and half the almonds. Turn into greased baking pan (9x13x2) and spread evenly. Sprinkle with remaining half cup almonds. Bake at 350 F about 30 minutes, til cookies test done. Cool in pan, then cut into bars. (Makes 2 dozen bars)

OATMEAL ROCKS

1½ cups quick cooking OATS
¼ cup MILK
1 cup sifted all-purpose FLOUR
1 teaspoon SALT
¾ teaspoon BAKING POWDER
¼ teaspoon NUTMEG
½ cup SHORTENING
¾ cup BROWN SUGAR (packed)
1 large EGG
1 teaspoon VANILLA
½ cup Sun-Maid ZANTE CURRANTS (orange box)
¼ cup chopped WALNUTS

Combine oats and milk. Let stand while preparing remaining ingredients. Resift flour with salt, baking powder and nutmeg. Cream shortening, sugar, egg and vanilla together well. Blend in flour mixture. Stir in oats, currants and walnuts; mix well. Drop by heaping teaspoonfuls onto greased baking sheets. Bake above center in 400 F oven about 10 minutes (til lightly browned). Let stand a minute, then remove to wire racks to cool. (Makes 2 dozen cookies, about 2 1/2'' in diameter.)

SOUR CREAM RAISIN PIE

1 unbaked 8-inch PIE SHELL
2 large EGGS
1 cup dairy SOUR CREAM
¾ cup SUGAR
1 teaspoon VANILLA
¼ teaspoon SALT
¼ teaspoon NUTMEG
1 cup Sun-Maid RAISINS (red box)
½ cup dairy SOUR CREAM

Prepare pie shell. Beat eggs, sour cream, sugar, vanilla, salt and nutmeg together until well blended. Stir in raisins. Pour into pastry shell. Bake below oven center in 375 F oven for 40 minutes (just til set). Cool. If desired, top each serving with spoonful of sour cream.

Standard Pie Crust

1 cup sifted all-purpose FLOUR
½ teaspoon SALT
1/3 cup SHORTENING
2 or 3 tablespoons cold MILK

Combine flour with salt. Cut in shortening til particles are size of peas. Sprinkle with cold milk to make a stiff dough. Roll on lightly floured board to fit into 8-inch pie pan. Fold edges under, and flute rim.

TRADITIONAL RAISIN STUFFING

1 cup thinly sliced CELERY
½ cup chopped ONION
½ cup BUTTER
½ cup WATER
1 chicken BOUILLON CUBE (crumbled)
¼ teaspoon SALT
¼ teaspoon PEPPER
1 teaspoon POULTRY SEASONING
1½ quarts coarse day-old BREAD CUBES (¼ inch)
¾ cup Sun-Maid Golden SEEDLESS RAISINS (gold box)

Saute celery and onion in butter til soft but not brown. Add water, bouillon cube, poultry seasoning, salt and pepper. Heat, stirring to mix well. Pour over bread cubes and raisins and mix lightly. Turn into buttered baking dish (or stuff into poultry for roasting). Bake at 350 F uncovered for 30 minutes (or til lightly toasted on top). (Makes 5 cups stuffing) To stuff a 12-to-15 pound turkey, double this recipe.

RAISIN BROWN BREAD

1 cup Calif. RAISINS
¾ cup CORN MEAL
¾ cup WHOLE WHEAT FLOUR (or graham flour)
1½ cups sifted all-purpose FLOUR
1½ teaspoons SALT
1½ teaspoons BAKING SODA
1 teaspoon BAKING POWDER
1 EGG (beaten)
1 cup BUTTERMILK (or sour milk)
¾ cup DARK MOLASSES
2 tablespoons VEGETABLE OIL

Combine raisins, corn meal and whole wheat flour. Sift together all-purpose flour, salt, soda and baking powder. Stir into raisin mixture. Combine egg, buttermilk, molasses and oil; stir into dry mixture just til moistened. Spoon batter into greased 10x5x3 loaf pan. Bake at 350 F for 50 minutes (or til pick inserted in center comes out clean). Cool in pan 10 minutes.

RAISIN CHEESECAKE

4 EGGS
1 cup SUGAR
¼ teaspoon SALT
1½ pounds (3 cups) RICOTTA CHEESE (or low fat cottage cheese, pressed through a fine sieve)
1 cup heavy (WHIPPING) CREAM
4 tablespoons sifted all purpose FLOUR
1 teaspoon VANILLA
3 tablespoons fresh LEMON JUICE
1 tablespoon grated fresh LEMON PEEL
½ cup seedless Calif. RAISINS

Press all but 3/4 cup of the crumbs firmly over bottom of a 9-inch spring-form pan. Bake in a 350 F oven for 15 minutes or til lightly browned. Cool on a rack. In a large mixing bowl, beat eggs til light-colored. Gradually add sugar, beating til mixture is thick and light. Thoroughly beat in salt and ricotta (or cottage cheese), then cream. Beat in flour, vanilla, and lemon juice. Fold in lemon peel and raisins. Pour over cooled crust. Sprinkle reserved crumbs evenly over top. Bake in a 350 F oven for 1 hour and 10 minutes (or til toothpick inserted in center comes out clean). Turn off oven and leave oven door open; allow cake to cool in oven for about 2 hours. Cover cake and chill. At serving time, remove sides of pan, and cut cake.

Cinnamon Crumb Crust

1 pkg. (6 oz.) ZWIEBACK
½ cup SUGAR
½ teaspoon CINNAMON
1/3 cup melted BUTTER

Whirl zwieback in a blender or crush by hand into fine crumbs. Mix well with sugar, cinnamon, and melted butter.

RAISIN GUMDROP COOKIES

3 cups sifted FLOUR
1 teaspoon BAKING SODA
1 teaspoon SALT
½ cup BUTTER
1/3 cup SUGAR
1 EGG
2/3 cup HONEY
1 teaspoon LEMON FLAVORING
1 cup RAISINS
½ cup very soft GUMDROPS (no licorice)

Sift together the flour, soda and salt and set aside. In a large bowl, cream together the butter and sugar. Add the egg, honey, and lemon flavoring. Stir in the raisins and gumdrops. Then add dry ingredients a little at a time, mixing well. Shape into a sausage roll 3 inches in diameter, and wrap in wax paper. Chill overnight. To bake, slice cookies with a sharp knife and place on a greased cookie sheet. (If dough becomes soft, put it back in refrigerator to chill.) Bake 8 to 10 minutes at 375 F.

CARROT-RAISIN SALAD

2/3 cup Calif. seedless RAISINS
2 cups grated CARROT
1 can PINEAPPLE TIDBITS
1/3 cup MAYONNAISE
1 tablespoon LEMON JUICE
¼ teaspoon SALT

Combine raisins, carrot and drained pineapple. Blend in mayonnaise, lemon juice and salt. Serve on crisp salad greens.

VELVETY RAISIN CHOPS

4 loin PORK CHOPS (1 inch thick)
2 tablespoons FLOUR
1 teaspoon SEASONED SALT
½ teaspoon DILL
2 tablespoons SHORTENING
¼ cup HONEY
½ cup ORANGE JUICE
½ cup LEMON JUICE
3 tablespoons TOMATO PASTE
½ cup Calif. seedless RAISINS
1 LEMON

Trim fat from chops. Blend flour with salt and dill weed; rub into chops. Brown chops slowly in shortening over moderate heat. Discard pan drippings. Combine honey, orange and lemon juices and pour over chops. Cover tightly; simmer over low heat 50 to 60 minutes* til almost tender. Blend tomato paste into pan sauce. Add raisins and thinly sliced lemon. Cover and continue cooking about 20 minutes longer, til meat is fork tender. (*Or bake at 375 F for an hour)

RAISIN CURRY

1 tablespoon CURRY POWDER
1 tablespoon BUTTER
1 sliced medium ONION
2 sliced medium stalks CELERY
1½ lbs. boneless lean LAMB
1 (14 oz.) can CHICKEN BROTH
1 teaspoon GARLIC SALT
2/3 cup Calif. seedless RAISINS
1½ tablespoons CORNSTARCH
2 tablespoons WATER

Combine curry, butter, onion, and celery. Cover and cook over moderate heat a few minutes, til vegetables wilt. Add lamb, (cut into small cubes), broth and salt. Cover tightly and simmer 1 to 1 1/2 hours, til meat is tender. Add raisins and cornstarch mixed with water. Cook slowly 15 minutes longer and serve over rice. (Makes 4 servings)

FRESNO RAISIN SAUCE

½ cup Calif. seedless RAISINS
¼ cup CIDER VINEGAR
¼ cup WATER
1 EGG
2 tablespoons DRY MUSTARD
½ cup BROWN SUGAR (packed)
¼ teaspoon SALT
1 teaspoon FLOUR
½ cup dairy SOUR CREAM

Heat coarsely chopped raisins, vinegar and water to simmering. Combine beaten egg with mustard, brown sugar, salt and flour. Add to raisin mixture. Cook, stirring over low heat, about 5 minutes til sauce thickens. Remove from heat and stir in sour cream. Serve hot with corned beef, ham or cold meats.

RAISIN RUM SAUCE

2 tablespoons BROWN SUGAR
1 tablespoon CORNSTARCH
½ cup WATER
½ cup ORANGE JUICE
1 tablespoon RUM
1/3 cup CURRANT JELLY
1 cup RAISINS
Pinch of Ground ALLSPICE
Pinch of SALT

Mix brown sugar and cornstarch in saucepan. Add water gradually, stirring until blended. Add remainder of ingredients. Cook over medium heat until clear and of a thick consistency. Serve as a sauce over baked ham.

Prunes

PRUNE FLUFF PIE

9 inch PASTRY SHELL (unbaked)
1 cup Del Monte PRUNES (cooked and pitted)
¾ cup chopped NUTS
½ cup SUGAR
1/8 teaspoon SALT
1½ teaspoon LEMON JUICE
1 teaspoon grated LEMON RIND
2 EGGS (separated)

Dice prunes. Combine with nuts, sugar, salt, lemon juice, lemon rind, and egg yolks. Mix well. Beat egg whites until stiff but not dry. Fold into prune mixture. Pour into pastry shell and bake at 325 F for 25 minutes.

PRUNE NUT BREAD

1 cup PRUNES
2 teaspoons shredded ORANGE PEEL
1 cup ORANGE JUICE
2 cups instant type FLOUR
¾ cup SUGAR
3 teaspoons BAKING POWDER
½ teaspoon SALT
½ teaspoon ground CINNAMON
2 EGGS
2 tablespoons SALAD OIL
½ cup chopped WALNUTS

Snip prunes into greased 9x5x3 pan. Add orange peel and juice. Let stand 1/2 hour. Add remaining ingredients and beat well with fork til blended (about 2 minutes). Scrape pan after beating one minute. Bake in 350 F oven for 55 minutes. Remove from pan and cool.

SAVORY PRUNE STUFFING

1 cup Del Monte PRUNES (cooked and pitted)
½ lb. ground PORK
½ cup chopped ONION
½ cup chopped CELERY
½ cup WATER
2 cups herb seasoned BREAD CUBES

Dice prunes. Brown meat. Add onion and celery and cook til tender. Stir in prunes and water. Toss meat mixture with bread cubes. Place in greased 1 1/2 quart baking dish. Cover and bake at 350 F for 25 minutes. (May be used to stuff 6 to 10 lb. poultry.) Yields 4 1/2 cups stuffing.

PRUNE SAUCE for Meatloaf

1 cup PRUNE JUICE
2 tablespoons ORANGE JUICE
2 teaspoons grated ORANGE PEEL
1½ tablespoons VINEGAR
½ cup BROWN SUGAR
1 tablespoon prepared MUSTARD
1 teaspoon CINNAMON
¼ teaspoon ALLSPICE
¼ teaspoon CLOVES
2 tablespoons BUTTER
2 tablespoons FLOUR

Combine prune juice,orange juice and peel, vinegar, sugar, mustard and spices. Heat. Combine butter and flour. Add to sauce and cook, stirring until thickened. Serve over meat loaf.

PRUNE LOAF

1½ cups SUGAR
2 tablespoons BUTTER
2 beaten EGG YOLKS
1 teaspoon BAKING POWDER
1½ teaspoon SODA
1 cup SOUR MILK
2 cups FLOUR
1 teaspoon VANILLA
1 cup STEWED PRUNES (pitted and mashed)
2 EGG WHITES

Cream sugar and butter til light and fluffy. Add yolks. Stir soda into sour milk. Sift baking powder and flour together. Alternately add milk and flour mixtures to creamed mixture. Add mashed prunes and vanilla and mix well. Fold in beaten egg whites and pour into two loaf pans, lightly greased. Bake at 350 F for 40 minutes (or til loaf is firm and leaves sides of pan). Remove from loaf pan when cool. Wrap and refrigerate. Slice when cold.

PRUNE SPICE CAKE

1 cup pitted PRUNES (cooked)
½ cup SHORTENING
1 cup SUGAR
1 EGG and 2 EGG YOLKS
2 cups sifted CAKE FLOUR
1 teaspoon SALT
1 teaspoon BAKING POWDER
1 teaspoon CINNAMON
½ teaspoon SODA
½ cup SOUR MILK (or buttermilk)

Cut prunes into small bits. Cream shortening and sugar thoroughly. Blend in well-beaten egg and yolks. Sift together flour, salt, baking powder, spice and soda. Add to creamed mixture alternately with buttermilk, beginning and ending with flour. Add prune bits and mix thoroughly. Pour into two greased 8-inch layer cake pans. Bake in 375 F oven 25 minutes (or til cake tests done). Cool and frost.

Brandy Frosting

2 cups (1 pint) WHIPPING CREAM
¼ cup Confectioners SUGAR
3 tablespoons BRANDY

Combine cream with confectioners sugar in small bowl and refrigerate for an hour. After chilling, beat til just stiff. Beat in brandy gradually. Frost layers, top and sides of cake. Refrigerate an hour or two before serving.

PRUNE-HONEY PUDDING

1 cup COOKED PRUNES (chopped)
½ cup HONEY
½ cup NUTS (chopped)
½ cup MILK
Grated RIND 1 LEMON
1 tablespoon BUTTER (melted)
½ cup soft BREAD CRUMBS
1 teaspoon BAKING POWDER

Mix all ingredients and pour into buttered 1-quart baking dish. Bake at 350 F for 30 minutes. Serve warm or cold with milk. (Serves 6)

Dates

DATE NUT BANANA BREAD

1¾ cups FLOUR
2 teaspoons BAKING POWDER
½ teaspoon BAKING SODA
½ teaspoon SALT
¾ cup SUGAR
½ cup SHORTENING
2 EGGS
1 cup mashed BANANAS
½ cup chopped DATES
½ cup chopped NUTS

Mix flour, baking powder, baking soda and salt thoroughly. In a separate bowl, mix sugar, shortening, and eggs til light and fluffy. Blend in mashed bananas, chopped dates, and nuts. Add dry ingredients and stir til smooth. Bake at 350 F in a 9x5 loaf pan for an hour (or til firmly set in center). Cool on rack for 10 minutes, and remove from pan.

INDIO DATE NUT BREAD

¾ cup chopped WALNUTS
1 cup cut-up pitted DATES
1½ teaspoons BAKING SODA
½ teaspoon SALT
3 tablespoons SHORTENING
1 cup canned APPLE SAUCE (heated)
2 EGGS
1 teaspoon VANILLA EXTRACT
1 cup granulated SUGAR
1½ cups sifted all-purpose FLOUR

With fork, mix walnuts, dates, baking soda and salt. Add shortening and applesauce. Let stand 20 minutes. Start heating oven to 350 F. Grease 9x5 inch loaf pan. With fork, beat eggs, beat in vanilla, sugar and flour. Mix in date mixture until just blended; turn into pan. Bake 1 hour and 5 minutes (or til cake tester inserted in center comes out clean). Cool in pan 10 minutes. Remove to wire rack to finish cooling. Then wrap in foil. Store overnight before slicing. Slices readily when frozen.

DATE CHEESE PUDDING

1 cup DATES
1 ORANGE
¼ cup RAW SUGAR (firmly packed)
2 tablespoons WATER
1 cup sifted whole wheat FLOUR
¼ teaspoon SALT
1 cup grated CHEDDAR CHEESE
¼ cup BUTTER

Chop dates. Cut orange into quarters and grind in food grinder. Combine dates, orange and raw sugar and spread in bottom of square baking pan. Sprinkle with water. Combine flour, salt and cheese. With a pastry blender or knife, cut butter into flour mixture til mixture is crumbly. Sprinkle over fruit mixture. Bake in 350 F oven 30 minutes.

DATE SHAKE

¾ cup chopped pitted DATES
1¼ cups MILK
1 pint VANILLA ICE CREAM

Put dates and 1/2 cup of milk in a blender and turn to high speed. Blend til mixture is almost smooth. Add the rest of the milk and the ice cream and blend on low speed til just mixed. Serve immediately in chilled glasses.

DATE WALNUT PIE

- 3 EGGS
- 1 cup dark or light CORN SYRUP
- 1 cup SUGAR
- 2 tablespoons MARGARINE (melted)
- 1 teaspoon VANILLA
- 1/8 teaspoon SALT
- 1 cup finely chopped DATES
- ½ cup WALNUT HALVES
- 1 unbaked (9 inch) PASTRY SHELL

Beat eggs slightly in large mixing bowl. Add corn syrup, sugar, margarine, vanilla and salt. Stir in dates and nuts. Pour into pastry shell and bake 15 minutes at 400 F. Reduce heat to 350 F and continue baking 35 minutes. (Filling should be less set in center than around edge of pie.)

CHOCOLATE CHIP DATE CAKE

- 1 cup chopped DATES
- 1 cup boiling WATER
- 2/3 cup SHORTENING
- 1 cup SUGAR
- 1 teaspoon VANILLA
- 2 EGGS
- 1¾ cup sifted CAKE FLOUR
- 2 tablespoons COCOA
- 1 teaspoon SODA
- ½ teaspoon SALT
- 1 pkg. (6 oz.) semi-sweet CHOCOLATE CHIPS
- 1 cup chopped NUTS

Combine dates and boiling water, and cool. Cream shortening and sugar, and blend in vanilla. Add eggs separately, beating well after each addition. Sift together dry ingredients. Add alternately with date mixture to creamed mixture. Spread in greased 13x9x2 pan. Sprinkle with chocolate chips. Bake at 350 F for 45 minutes. Cool in pan.

DATE PUDDING

- ½ cup SUGAR
- 1 EGG (beaten)
- 1 cup DATES
- ½ cup WALNUTS
- ¼ cup FLOUR
- ½ teaspoon SALT
- ½ teaspoon BAKING POWDER

Mix sugar and eggs thoroughly. Add remaining ingredients. Pour into greased shallow baking dish. Bake at 350 F for 30 minutes. Serve warm or cold with hard sauce or cream.

DATE CLUSTERS

- 2 cups DATES
- ½ cup SHORTENING
- 1 cup SUGAR
- 1 EGG
- 1 teaspoon VANILLA
- 2 cups sifted FLOUR
- 1 teaspoon SALT
- ½ teaspoon BAKING SODA
- ½ cup BUTTERMILK

Cut dates into small pieces. Cream shortening with sugar. Beat in eggs and vanilla. Sift flour with salt and soda. Blend alternately into creamed mixture with buttermilk. Stir in dates. Drop by teaspoonfuls onto greased baking sheet. Bake in 375 F oven for 10 minutes (or til lightly browned at edges). (Makes 5 dozen cookies)

DATE FRUITCAKE

4 cups DATES (pitted, whole)
1 lb. WALNUT MEATS (whole)
½ lb. each CANDIED CHERRIES and PINEAPPLE
1 cup FLOUR
½ teaspoon SALT
3 teaspoons BAKING POWDER
1 cup SUGAR
4 EGGS (separated)

Sift the flour, salt and baking powder and mix with fruits and nuts. Then add sugar and mix. Next add egg yolks (well beaten). Mix well. Add egg whites (which must be beaten stiff and dry) and vanilla. Put into two loaf pans which have been lined with wax paper, and buttered and floured. Bake one hour at 350 F.

DATE BRAN MUFFINS

¼ cup soft SHORTENING (or butter)
¼ cup HONEY
1 EGG
¾ cup MILK
1 cup WHOLE BRAN
1 cup PITTED DATES (snipped)
1 cup sifted all purpose FLOUR
2 teaspoons BAKING POWDER
½ teaspoon SALT

Cream together shortening and honey. Add egg, beat well. Stir in milk, bran and dates. Sift together dry ingredients. Add to date mixture. Stir just to moisten ingredients. Batter will look lumpy. Grease 12 muffin pan cups (2 1/2 inch size). Fill 2/3 full. Heat oven to 400 F. Bake for 20 minutes til done.

DATE-WINE BARS

1 cup DATES (finely cut)
1 cup SUGAR
½ cup Calif. SHERRY
¼ cup WATER
1 tablespoon LEMON JUICE
1 teaspoon LEMON RIND
1 cup chopped NUTS
1 cup BROWN SUGAR
¼ teaspoon SALT
1 teaspoon BAKING SODA
1¾ cups quick-cooking OATS
1½ cups FLOUR
½ cup BUTTER

Combine dates, sugar, sherry and water in saucepan. Bring to boil. Reduce heat and simmer, stirring frequently, until mixture is thick. Remove from heat. Add lemon juice, rind, and nuts and cool. Mix dry ingredients. Add butter to make a crumb mixture. Spread half of crumbs firmly into greased 8" square pan. Spread cooled date mixture evenly over crumbs. Cover with remaining crumbs. Bake at 350 F for 30 minutes. Cool in pan and cut into squares. (Makes 16 pieces)

DATE WAFFLES

2 cups FLOUR
½ teaspoon SALT
2 teaspoons BAKING POWDER
¼ cup BUTTER
2 cups MILK
2 EGGS
1 cup Calif. DATES (chopped)

Sift together flour, salt and baking powder, add yolks of eggs, butter and milk gradually and beat til perfectly smooth. Add dates and whites of eggs, beaten til stiff, and bake as ordinary waffles. Serve with butter and honey. (Serves six)

FIG HEALTH SALAD

2 cups shredded CABBAGE
2 cups shredded raw CARROTS
½ cup chopped NUTS
2 large diced APPLES
1 cup thinly sliced Calif. DRIED FIGS

Toss all ingredients together and serve with favorite dressing.

PORTUGUESE HAM SKILLET

1 (1 lb.) sliced fully cooked HAM
2 tablespoons BUTTER
1 cup sliced Calif. DRIED FIGS
2 tablespoons BROWN SUGAR
1/8 teaspoon ground CLOVES
¼ teaspoon DRY MUSTARD
1/3 cup PORT WINE

Lightly saute ham on both sides in skillet with butter. Stir in figs, brown sugar, cloves, mustard and wine. Cover and simmer 10 minutes.

TERIYAKI LAMB KABOBS

½ cup PINEAPPLE JUICE
¼ cup SOY SAUCE
2 tablespoons BROWN SUGAR
¼ teaspoon GINGER
1/8 teaspoon GARLIC SALT
1½ lbs. boned LAMB SHOULDER (cut into cubes)
6 slices BACON
6 slices canned PINEAPPLE (drained)
12 Calif. DRIED FIGS
Cooked RICE

Combine pineapple juice with soy, brown sugar, ginger, and garlic salt. Make kabobs by combining alternately on skewers: lamb, bacon, pineapple and figs. Place kabobs in shallow pan. Pour pineapple marinade over kabobs and refrigerate for several hours. Drain kabobs, reserving marinade. Broil for about 10 minutes, brushing occasionally with sauce. Turn and broil 10 minutes longer. Serve on hot rice. (Makes 6 servings)

GLAZED GOURMET FIGS

24 Calif. DRIED FIGS
3 cups cold WATER
¼ cup CIDER VINEGAR
1 teaspoon whole CLOVES
1 cup Calif. BRANDY
1 tablespoon WHITE CORN SYRUP
24 lightly browned ALMONDS

Place figs and water in saucepan. Bring to hard boil, then lower heat to simmer. Cover and let cook 20 minutes. Add all ingredients except almonds. Stir gently in order not to break figs. Cover and simmer again for about 20 minutes or til figs are plump and transparent. Cool in syrup. Add a little water, if needed, but keep it rich. Just before serving, insert toasted almond in each fig. (Serve with roast turkey, or baked chicken, beef, pork, or ham.)

FIG MINI COFFEE CAKES

10 stewed and drained Calif. DRIED FIGS
2 EGGS
½ cup SUGAR
½ cup MILK
3 tablespoons melted SHORTENING
1½ cups sifted all purpose FLOUR
½ teaspoon SALT
2 teaspoons BAKING POWDER

Topping

½ cup BROWN SUGAR
1 tablespoon FLOUR
1 teaspoon CINNAMON
3 tablespoons melted BUTTER (or margarine)
Chopped WALNUT MEATS

Snip stems from figs, cut them into small bits. Combine figs, eggs, sugar, milk, shortening. Beat together until well mixed. Sift flour, measure and sift again with salt and baking powder. Add to first mixture, stir til just mixed. Place paper baking cups into muffin tins. Spoon batter into cups, filling them half full. Sprinkle with topping. Bake at 375 F for about 15 minutes or til light brown and firm to touch. (Makes 16 cakes.)

FIG FRUIT CAKE

20 Calif. DRIED FIGS
½ lb. CANDIED CHERRIES
¼ lb. CANDIED PINEAPPLE
2½ cups chopped WALNUTS
1 cup sifted CAKE FLOUR
1 teaspoon SALT
1½ teaspoons BAKING POWDER
1 teaspoon each: CINNAMON and ALLSPICE
½ teaspoon CLOVES
½ cup SHORTENING
1½ cups SUGAR
5 EGGS (separated)
2 squares BAKING CHOCOLATE, melted
4 tablespoons BRANDY (or water)
1½ teaspoons VANILLA
1 teaspoon ALMOND EXTRACT

Butter a 6x10x3 loaf pan. Line with waxed paper and butter generously again. Set oven for 250 F. Cover figs with very hot water, and let stand 10 minutes, then drain. With scissors, snip off stems. Then cut figs, cherries and pineapple into tiny bits. Add chopped nuts and half the sifted flour. Mix together lightly. Sift remaining flour with salt, baking powder and spices. Cream shortening, sugar, egg yolks and melted chocolate. Whip egg whites til very light. Combine all ingredients til just mixed. Place in greased baking pan and bake in slow oven 250F for about 3 to 4 hours. Place pan of hot water in bottom of oven during baking. When cool, brush with hot corn syrup and decorate with figs, candied fruit and nuts.

STEWED FIGS

Rinse and drain figs, cover generously with water. Cover pan and cook slowly over low heat 35 minutes. (Sugar may be added after cooking, if desired).

Variations: add one teaspoon of lemon juice for every 4 or 5 figs, with a piece of lemon rind. Simmer 5 minutes more and serve either warm or chilled.

PEANUT BUTTER FIG CRUNCHIES

¾ cup BUTTER (or margarine)
¾ cup SUGAR
½ cup BROWN SUGAR
2/3 cup PEANUT BUTTER
1 EGG (slightly beaten)
1 teaspoon VANILLA
1¾ cup FLOUR
½ teaspoon SODA
½ teaspoon SALT
SUGAR
1 cup chopped Calif. DRIED FIGS

Cream butter and sugars. Blend in peanut butter, egg, and vanilla. Add sifted flour, soda, salt and figs. Mix well. Form into small balls; roll in sugar. Bake on ungreased cookie sheets at 375 F for 10-12 minutes. (Makes about 60 cookies)

FIG OATMEAL COOKIES

1 cup Calif. DRIED FIGS (coarsely chopped)
¾ cup SHORTENING
1 cup BROWN SUGAR
2 EGGS
8 tablespoons WATER
2 cups FLOUR
2 teaspoons BAKING POWDER
1 teaspoon CINNAMON
½ teaspoon SALT
2 cups quick cooking OATS
½ cup chopped NUT MEATS

Cover figs with hot water, allow to stand 10 minutes. Pour off water and reserve for liquid. Snip stems off figs, then chop coarsely. Sift flour, measure. Then add baking powder, salt, and cinnamon. Sift together. Add oats, chopped figs and nuts. Cream shortening; add sugar, cream together thoroughly. Add well-beaten eggs, then add sifted dry ingredients alternately with water to form dough. Drop by teaspoonfuls on greased cookie sheet and bake at 400 F for 10 minutes. (Makes 48 cookies)

FIG BREAD

1 ORANGE (unpeeled)
8 Calif. DRIED FIGS
2½ cups sifted FLOUR
1 teaspoon SALT
½ teaspoon SODA
1½ teaspoons BAKING POWDER
2 EGGS
2/3 cup SUGAR
1 cup WATER
1/3 cup melted BUTTER (or margarine)
½ cup chopped WALNUTS

Cut orange into quarters. Put figs and orange through food chopper. Sift flour with salt, soda and baking powder. Beat eggs just enough to mix well; stir in sugar, water, butter and fig-orange mixture. Add dry ingredients and nuts. Stir just enough to blend. Spoon into lightly greased and floured loaf pan. Bake at 350 F for 60-70 minutes.

SHERRIED FIGS

Fill a bowl with California dried figs and cover with California sherry. Turn occasionally, so figs are well soaked. Let stand for 24 hours or longer. Drain and roll in confectioners sugar.

Avocados

GUACAMOLE (Avocado Dip)

In making this traditional appetizer, the avocados may be mashed for the coarse texture that is traditionally Mexican, or pureed for a smooth texture. When covering guacamole, place plastic wrap directly on dip to keep color fresh.

2 Calif. AVOCADOS
2 tablespoons fresh LEMON (or lime) JUICE
2 small green ONIONS (chopped)
½ teaspoon SALT
Dash of WORCESTERSHIRE or Tabasco

Mash avocado and add seasonings, or combine all ingredients in blender. Makes about one cup dip. (Mix just before serving)

...with TOMATOES

2 AVOCADOS (mashed or pureed)
¼ cup SOUR CREAM
2 tablespoons MINCED ONION
2 teaspoons SALT
1 teaspoon CHILI POWDER
1 clove GARLIC (crushed)
Dash TABASCO
4 teaspoons LEMON JUICE
2 medium TOMATOES (peeled and chopped)

Combine all ingredients. Cover and chill. (Makes about 3 cups)

...with GREEN CHILI PEPPERS

4 AVOCADOS (mashed or pureed)
½ cup finely chopped canned GREEN CHILI PEPPERS
¼ cup minced ONION
1 tablespoon SALT
¼ cup LEMON JUICE

CLASSIC AVOCADO SALAD

½ head BOSTON LETTUCE
½ head ROMAINE
½ head CHICORY
½ pint CHERRY TOMATOES (halved)
2 AVOCADOS (peeled and sliced)
3 slices BACON (cooked and crumbled)
3 oz. crumbled ROQUEFORT (or blue cheese)

Into large salad bowl tear greens in bite-sized pieces. Add tomatoes and avocados. Sprinkle with bacon and cheese. Toss lightly with Herb Dressing.

Herb Dressing

1 cup Vegetable OIL
6 tablespoons WINE VINEGAR
¼ cup LEMON JUICE
1 teaspoon SALT
1 teaspoon SUGAR
½ teaspoon BASIL LEAVES
2 cloves GARLIC (crushed)
Dash PEPPER

Combine all ingredients and chill, covered. (Makes 1 1/2 cups)

AVOCADO SALSAS (Avocado Relish)

...for Grilled Meats, Game or Fowl

2 fully ripe Calif. AVOCADOS
2 large TOMATOES (peeled and chopped)
1 each: RED ONION and GREEN PEPPER (coarsely chopped)
1 GREEN CHILI (minced)
1 teaspoon SALT
Dash black PEPPER
2 tablespoons LEMON JUICE

Halve avocados lengthwise, twisting gently to separate halves. Peel avocado halves; place cavity-side down and dice; then toss with remaining ingredients and chill. Serve as side dish.

...for Baked or Grilled Fish

2 AVOCADOS (diced)
¼ cup BUTTER (½ stick)
2 tablespoons finely chopped ONION
¼ cup FLOUR
1 teaspoon SALT
2 cups WATER
1 cup SOUR CREAM
2 teaspoons prepared HORSERADISH

In saucepan, saute onion in butter until crisp-tender. Quickly stir in flour and salt. Gradually stir in water, til sauce boils one minute. Remove from heat and stir in sour cream, horseradish and avocado; heat gently. (Makes about 5 cups)

...for Cold Meats & Seafood

2 AVOCADOS (diced)
¼ cup each: CHIVES, PARSLEY, WATERCRESS (all chopped)
1 tablespoon SALT
1 cup LEMON JUICE
1 cup SOUR CREAM
¼ cup MAYONNAISE
4 teaspoons ANCHOVY PASTE
2 dashes TABASCO

Whirl all ingredients in electric blender; chill. (Makes 5 cups)

AVOCADO LEMON BUTTER

1 AVOCADO (pureed)
Juice of 1 LEMON
1 lb. SWEET BUTTER (softened)

Combine avocado puree and lemon juice. Beat with butter until blended. (Makes about 4 cups).

AVOCADO HERB BUTTER

1 AVOCADO (pureed)
1 lb. SWEET BUTTER (softened)
2 tablespoons chopped PARSLEY
½ teaspoon each: OREGANO LEAVES, ground SAVORY
¼ teaspoon TARRAGON LEAVES
2 tablespoons LEMON JUICE

Whip together all ingredients til light and fluffy. (Makes 4 cups)

AVOCADO PUREE

Mash peeled avocado with fork or force through sieve or food mill or puree in electric mixer or blender. Blend by portions when working with large amounts.

AVOCADO PIE

1 prepared 8-inch CRUMB CRUST
1 14-oz. can sweetened CONDENSED MILK
1 cup mashed (or pureed) Calif. AVOCADO
½ cup reconstituted LIME JUICE
½ teaspoon SALT

In large bowl, combine sweetened condensed milk, avocados, lime juice and salt; blend well. Turn into prepared crust. Chill. Garnish with slices of avocado and whipped topping.

AVOCADO LIME PIE

1 AVOCADO (pureed with ½ cup fresh lime juice, about 5 limes)
1½ cups SUGAR
1/3 cup CORNSTARCH
¼ teaspoon SALT
1½ cups WATER
4 EGG YOLKS (beaten)
1 tablespoon grated LIME PEEL
9" baked PIE SHELL

In saucepan blend: sugar, cornstarch and salt; gradually stir in water. Stir to boil over medium heat and boil 1/2 minute. Gradually beat half of hot mixture into egg yolks; then return to saucepan. Stir and boil one minute longer. Remove from heat and stir in lime peel. Blend in avocado puree. Turn into pie shell. Top with meringue. Bake in 350 F oven 10 to 15 minutes til golden brown. (Lemon peel and lemon juice may be substituted for lime. For individual desserts, avocado filling may be turned into 8 tart shells.)

Meringue

4 EGG WHITES (room temperature)
¼ teaspoon CREAM of TARTAR
1/8 teaspoon SALT
½ cup SUGAR

Beat egg whites (at room temperature), cream of tartar and salt until foamy. Continue beating, gradually adding sugar, til stiff, but not dry. Pile on pie and bake.

AVOCADO CHIFFON PIE

1 AVOCADO (pureed with ½ cup fresh lime juice, about 5 limes)
1 cup SUGAR
1 envelope unflavored GELATINE
¼ teaspoon SALT
3 EGGS (separated, at room temperature)
½ cup MILK
1 tablespoon grated LIME PEEL
9-inch baked PIE SHELL
Sweetened WHIPPED CREAM (for garnish)

In top of double boiler, combine 1/2 cup sugar, gelatine and salt. Beat egg yolks lightly with milk and stir in. Stir over boiling water until gelatine dissolves (about 5 minutes). Remove from heat; stir in lime peel, then avocado puree. Chill til mixture mounds slightly when dropped from a spoon. Beat egg white, gradually adding remaining 1/2 cup sugar, til stiff, but not dry. Fold into avocado mixture; turn into baked 9" pie shell. Chill til firm.

AVOCADO SOUP--California Style

2 tablespoons OIL
½ cup diced CELERY
½ cup diced ONIONS
½ cup diced BELL PEPPER
1 clove GARLIC
¼ teaspoon CHILI POWDER
¼ teaspoon OREGANO
1 tablespoon fresh CILANTRO
5 cups WATER
1 tablespoon CHICKEN BOUILLON POWDER
¼ cup raw RICE
1 tablespoon chopped PIMIENTOS
½ cup GREEN CHILI SALSA
½ cup GARBANZO BEANS
1½ teaspoons CORNSTARCH
1 diced Calif. AVOCADO

Saute celery, onions, pepper and garlic in oil til transparent. Add chili powder, oregano, cilantro and cook for 2 minutes. Add water and let come to a boil. Add all other ingredients, except cornstarch and diced California avocado. Cook for 25 minutes on a low simmer. Thicken soup with cornstarch dissolved in warm water. Simmer 5 minutes more. Serve, garnishing each bowl with diced avocado. (Serves 8)

PONDEROSA SOUP

3 AVOCADOS
3 cups CHICKEN BROTH (or bouillon)
1½ CUCUMBERS (peeled and sliced)
¾ cup SOUR CREAM
3 tablespoons LEMON JUICE
1½ teaspoons SALT
Dash TABASCO
3 large TOMATOES (peeled and diced)

Puree avocados with all ingredients except tomatoes. Chill thoroughly, then garnish with tomatoes. (Serves 6)

LEMON TREE SOUP

3 AVOCADOS
¾ cup LEMON JUICE
3 cups VEGETABLE BOUILLON
1½ cups SOUR CREAM
1½ teaspoons SALT

Puree avocados with lemon juice and bouillon. Add half of the sour cream and salt, and after chilling thoroughly, garnish with the remainder. (Serves 6)

AVOCADO SOUP with GARLIC

4 fully ripe Calif. AVOCADOS
2 cups CHICKEN BROTH
2 teaspoons LIME JUICE
½ teaspoon SALT
1/8 teaspoon GARLIC POWDER
2 cups heavy CREAM

Halve avocados lengthwise, twisting gently to separate halves. Lift seed out and peel avocado halves. Puree in electric blender with broth, lime juice, salt and garlic powder. Stir in cream. Chill thoroughly. Garnish with lemon slices or with heavy cream, whipped with a dash of garlic powder.

AVOCADO on the HALF SHELL

Use 3 or 4 avocados in unpeeled halves to fill with any of the following (to serve 6 or 8)

...with TOMATO SALSA

6 medium TOMATOES (coarsely chopped)
9 green ONIONS (chopped)
1½ tablespoons chopped PARSLEY
¾ teaspoon BASIL LEAVES
¼ teaspoon ROSEMARY LEAVES
1/3 cup bottled ITALIAN DRESSING

Combine and chill all ingredients. Spoon into avocado halves.

...with GREEN SAUCE (Salsa Verde)

¼ cup each: finely choppea GREEN PEPPER, PARSLEY
2 tablespoons finely chopped CELERY
1 tablespoon each: finely chopped SCALLIONS, PIMIENTO, drained CAPERS
1 teaspoon finely chopped ANCHOVY FILLETS
½ teaspoon SALT
1/8 teaspoon each: PEPPER, BASIL
½ cup OLIVE OIL (or salad oil)

Combine and chill all ingredients. Spoon into avocado halves.

...with GARLIC SALSA

3 cloves GARLIC (crushed)
1 tablespoon BASIL LEAVES
¼ teaspoon SALT
1/8 teaspoon WHITE PEPPER
2 tablespoons grated PARMESAN CHEESE
½ cup OLIVE OIL (or salad oil)
2 tablespoons WINE VINEGAR

Combine and chill all ingredients. Spoon into avocado halves.

...with TARTAR STEAK

3 or 4 AVOCADOS (halved and peeled)
2 pounds twice-ground SIRLOIN
½ cup minced ONION
¼ cup chopped PARSLEY
1½ teaspoons SALT
6 to 8 unbroken EGG YOLKS

Mix together beef, onion, parsley and salt; fill half shells. Make indentations in centers; add egg yolks. Garnish with choice of: capers, cracked pepper, lemon wedges, dill pickle.

...with SHRIMP

2 cups cooked SHRIMP
2 tablespoons chopped CELERY
2 tablespoons chopped ONION
¼ cup MAYONNAISE
1/8 teaspoon PEPPER
1/8 teaspoon SALT
2 Calif. AVOCADOS

Mix shrimp, celery, onion, mayonnaise or salad dressing, salt and pepper to blend. Chill. Just before serving time, halve and remove seed from avocados. Spoon 1/2 cup shrimp mixture over each avocado half shell. Serve immediately.

RIPE OLIVE BEEF TACOS

1 pound lean GROUND BEEF
1 tablespoon COOKING OIL
¾ cup chopped ONION
1 minced clove GARLIC
1 teaspoon SALT
2 finely chopped canned GREEN CHILES
1 (No. 1) can pitted Calif. OLIVES (chopped)
1 (8 oz.) can TOMATO SAUCE
8 corn TORTILLAS
Shredded iceberg LETTUCE
Shredded JACK CHEESE
Sliced Calif. AVOCADO

Brown beef in one tablespoon cooking oil, adding onion and garlic when meat is about half cooked. Add salt, chiles, coarsely chopped ripe olives and tomato sauce. Cook very slowly about five minutes. Meanwhile, fry tortillas lightly in oil. Fold in half, holding with fork to shape. Drain well. Fill tortillas with ripe olive mixture. Add lettuce, cheese and avocado as desired.

OLIVE SWISS STEAK

3 lbs. TOP ROUND (1¼ inches thick)
2 tablespoons FLOUR
½ teaspoon SALT
1/8 teaspoon PEPPER
2 tablespoons COOKING OIL
¾ cup chopped ONION
¾ teaspoon minced GARLIC
¼ cup chopped GREEN PEPPER
1 cup canned TOMATO SAUCE
1/3 cup LIQUID (from olives)
¾ teaspoon CHILI POWDER
¼ teaspoon OREGANO
1 cup Lindsay Pitted Ripe OLIVES

Trim off excess fat from meat. Cut beef into six serving pieces. Combine flour, salt, pepper. Coat meat with mixture. Heat oil, add meat and brown. Put meat in a baking dish. Preheat oven to 350 F. Add onion, garlic and green pepper to oil and saute lightly. Add all remaining ingredients to onion mixture and bring to boil. Pour over meat. Cover and bake about 2 1/2 hours (or til meat is tender). (Makes 6 servings)

OLIVE-STUFFED FLANK STEAK

1 FLANK STEAK
SALT, PEPPER, FLOUR
4 cups BREAD CUBES
1 medium ONION (chopped)
¼ cup chopped CELERY
½ cup Lindsay Chopped Ripe OLIVES
1½ teaspoons SAGE
3 tablespoons BUTTER

Have flank steak scored lightly crosswise by butcher. Sprinkle with salt and pepper, dredge with flour and pound well with potato masher. Combine bread cubes, onions, celery, chopped olives, sage and butter. Moisten with water and season with salt and pepper. Spread stuffing over flank steak, roll meat and tie or fasten edge with toothpicks. Brown in fat. Transfer to baking dish, add 1/2 cup water, cover pan and bake at 350 F for 1 1/2 hours (or til tender).

OLIVE CORNISH HENS

- 6 Cornish GAME HENS
- 2 cups WATER
- ½ cup Lindsay Pitted Ripe OLIVES
- ½ cup ONION (chopped)
- ½ cup CELERY (chopped)
- ½ cup BUTTER (softened)
- 1 cup Lindsay Chopped Ripe OLIVES
- 3 cups soft BREAD CRUMBS
- ½ teaspoon SALT
- ¼ teaspoon THYME
- ¼ teaspoon PEPPER
- 2 tablespoons minced ONION
- 2 tablespoons FLOUR
- 2 tablespoons dry SHERRY
- 2 tablespoons minced PARSLEY

Thaw hens; clean cavities. Simmer giblets in water til tender. Preheat oven to 425 F. Cook chopped onion and celery in 1/4 cup butter. Add chopped olives, bread crumbs, salt, thyme, pepper. Stuff lightly into hens. Truss and brush with butter. Put in shallow baking pan for one hour, basting often with butter. Remove to platter. Cook minced onion in 2 tablespoons butter. Blend in flour. Gradually add 1 1/2 cups broth from giblets. Cook, stirring until thickened. Add giblets, sherry, parsley and reserved 1/2 cup pitted olives. Serve as gravy with hens.

OLIVE RICE PILAF

- ¾ cup Lindsay Chopped Ripe OLIVES
- 1/3 cup chopped ONION
- 3 tablespoons BUTTER
- 1¼ cup long grain RICE
- 2½ cups CHICKEN BROTH
- ½ teaspoon SALT
- ¼ teaspoon DILL
- ¼ teaspoon PEPPER
- 2 tablespoons PARSLEY (chopped)
- 2 tablespoons PIMIENTO (chopped)

Saute olives and onion in butter til onion is transparent. Add rice and cook about five minutes, stirring frequently. Add broth, salt, dill and pepper. Heat to boiling. Cover; cook over low heat for 20 minutes. Add parsley and chopped pimiento and stir lightly with fork. (Makes 6 servings)

BARBECUE SAUCE

- ¼ cup BUTTER
- 1 tablespoon FLOUR
- 1 clove GARLIC (minced)
- 2 cups TOMATO JUICE
- 3 tablespoons LEMON JUICE
- 1 tablespoon WORCESTERSHIRE SAUCE
- 2 tablespoons BROWN SUGAR
- 1 teaspoon DRY MUSTARD
- 1 teaspoon CHILI POWDER
- 1 teaspoon SALT
- 1/3 cup Lindsay Chopped Ripe OLIVES
- ¼ cup chopped ONION

Melt butter; stir in flour and garlic. Add tomato juice. Cook and stir a few minutes. Mix in remaining ingredients except olives and simmer 15 minutes. Add olives to sauce. Simmer five minutes. (Makes about 2 cups) Use to baste barbecued meats, poultry, or fish.

EGGPLANT SAN JOAQUIN

1 large EGGPLANT (diced)
1 cup Lindsay Pitted Ripe OLIVES
½ cup grated PARMESAN CHEESE
1 (No. 2½) can TOMATOES
1 large ONION (sliced)
SALT and PEPPER
Pinch of BASIL

Combine eggplant, tomatoes and onion in a heavy skillet. Stir in salt and pepper to taste, and basil. Cook over low heat covered, til eggplant is tender, 20 to 30 minutes. Stir in cheese and ripe olives just before eggplant is completely cooked.

OLIVE PASTA

1 (6 oz.) pkg. medium wide NOODLES
Boiling SALTED WATER
4 tablespoons BUTTER
1 tablespoon FLOUR
1 cup MILK
½ teaspoon SALT
1/8 teaspoon NUTMEG
Dash PEPPER
3 tablespoons grated PARMESAN CHEESE
1 cup small curd COTTAGE CHEESE
½ cup dairy SOUR CREAM
1 tablespoon minced ONION
2 tablespoons chopped GREEN PEPPER
2 tablespoons chopped PIMIENTO
1 EGG YOLK
1 can Lindsay Pitted Ripe OLIVES
1½ cups soft BREAD CRUMBS

Cook noodles in boiling salted water according to package directions. Melt 1 tablespoon butter and blend in flour. Add milk, salt, nutmeg and pepper. Cook, stirring, until sauce boils thoroughly. Stir in cheeses, sour cream, onion, green pepper, pimiento and egg yolk. Toss lightly with drained noodles and ripe olives cut into halves. Turn into buttered 1 1/2 quart baking dish. Melt remaining 3 tablespoons butter and mix with crumbs. Sprinkle over noodles. Bake at 350 F for 25 minutes.

OLIVE MACARONI LOAF

1½ cups Elbow MACARONI
1 cup soft BREAD CRUMBS
1 cup grated CHEESE
1½ cups MILK
4 EGGS (beaten in milk)
1 PIMIENTO (chopped)
1 cup Lindsay Pitted Ripe OLIVES
1 ONION (chopped)
1 tablespoon PARSLEY

Cook macaroni til tender and drain. Mix ingredients together with macaroni. Place in loaf pan and bake at 350 F 45 minutes.

Mushroom Sauce

1 can MUSHROOM SOUP
1 can MUSHROOMS (small)
1 tablespoon FLOUR
½ cup WATER

Blend all ingredients, bring to boil, simmer and serve over macaroni loaf.

OLIVE BEEF BIRDS

- 2 pounds ROUND STEAK
- 4 tablespoons BUTTER (bacon fat)
- 1 medium ONION (minced)
- 1 cup BREAD CRUMBS
- 1 cup Lindsay Chopped Ripe OLIVES
- ½ teaspoon CELERY SALT
- 1 teaspoon minced PARSLEY
- SALT and PEPPER
- FLOUR
- 1 cup CONSOMME

Buy thinly sliced meat and have butcher flatten it with his cleaver. Salt lightly and cut in uniform strips (about 3x5). Make stuffing by melting fat in a skillet and adding onions. Saute til light brown. Then blend in bread crumbs, parsley, celery salt and cup of ripe olives. Taste for seasoning, add more salt as needed and dash of pepper. Spread a spoonful of stuffing on meat strips, roll up, and fasten with skewer or toothpick. Sprinkle rolls with flour and brown on all sides. Pack closely in a shallow casserole. Add consomme til liquid comes halfway to top of beef rolls. Cover and bake in 350 F oven til meat is tender (about one hour). (Makes 4 servings)

SPAGHETTI SAUCE

- 1 lb. ground lean BEEF
- ¼ cup OLIVE OIL
- 1 large ONION
- 1 clove GARLIC
- 1/3 cup chopped GREEN PEPPER
- 3½ cups canned TOMATOES (no. 2½ can)
- ½ BAY LEAF
- 2 teaspoons SALT
- 1 teaspoon CHILI POWDER
- ½ teaspoon BASIL
- ¼ teaspoon BLACK PEPPER
- 1 cup Lindsay Pitted Ripe OLIVES

Brown meat in olive oil. Chop onion and mince garlic. Add with green pepper to meat and cook til lightly browned. Stir in tomatoes and seasonings and simmer one hour or longer. (If sauce becomes too thick, add water as needed). Quarter half of olives and add with remaining olives to sauce a few minutes before serving, heating thoroughly. (Makes 6 servings)

SHERRY OLIVE SAUCE

- 1 (4 oz.) can sliced MUSHROOMS
- 3 tablespoons FLOUR
- ¼ cup BUTTER
- ¾ cup MEAT STOCK
- 1 tablespoon chopped ONION
- 2½ tablespoons chopped GREEN PEPPER
- ¼ cup Lindsay Chopped Ripe OLIVES
- SALT and PEPPER
- 1 tablespoon SHERRY

Drain mushrooms and measure 1/4 cup liquid. Brown flour in 3 tablespoons butter; add meat stock and liquid from mushrooms; cook til thickened, stirring constantly. Saute onion and green pepper in remaining butter and add to sauce. Add ripe olives, season with salt and pepper. Simmer 10 or 12 minutes. Remove from heat and add sherry. (Makes 1 1/2 cups)

SAN JOAQUIN MELON SALAD

1 medium CANTALOUPE
2 cups cooked CHICKEN
2 cups seedless GRAPES
1½ cups diced CELERY
¼ cup rich MILK
2 teaspoons CURRY POWDER
2 tablespoons CHUTNEY (chopped)
¼ teaspoon SALT
1 cup MAYONNAISE

Cut melon into 4 wedges. Remove seeds. Run sharp knife between melon flesh and rind from one tip almost to the other. Cut chicken in bite-sized pieces; combine chicken with grapes and celery. Add milk, curry, chutney and salt to mayonnaise and blend. Pour dressing over chicken and chill. Serve chicken salad on melon wedges. Garnish with parsley. (Makes 4 servings)

CANTALOUPE WALDORF SALAD

2 cups CANTALOUPE CUBES (2 small melons)
1½ cups ORANGE SECTIONS
¾ cup seeded GRAPES
¾ cup diced CELERY
10 DATES (pitted and sliced)
½ cup WALNUTS (broken)

Toss ingredients together and chill. Serve in crisp iceberg lettuce cups, and top with dressing. (Serves 4)

Cream Cheese Dressing

1 3-oz. pkg. CREAM CHEESE
1½ tablespoons LEMON JUICE
3 tablespoons CURRANT JELLY
½ cup heavy CREAM (whipped)

Soften cream cheese; add lemon juice and currant jelly and beat til smooth. Fold in whipped cream and chill.

CALIFORNIA FRUIT COMBO

1 head western iceberg LETTUCE
1 can (1 lb.) CLING PEACH slices
2 BANANAS
½ cup pitted Calif. DATES
1 cup MELON BALLS (fresh or frozen)
3 tablespoons ORANGE MARMALADE
3 tablespoons WINE VINEGAR
1/3 cup CORN OIL
¼ teaspoon SALT
Dash WHITE PEPPER

Core, rinse and drain lettuce thoroughly; chill in disposable plastic bag. Line shallow salad bowl with outer lettuce leaves. Cut remaining lettuce into 1-inch cube-like chunks. Drain the peaches. Slice bananas diagonally. Cut dates lengthwise into halves. Arrange lettuce chunks and fruits in bowl. Combine remaining ingredients in bottle or jar; cover and shake well. Drizzle over lettuce and fruit mixture. (Makes 6 servings)

MELON SCOOP SALAD

Line a salad bowl with fresh greens. Fill center with equal parts of cantaloupe and watermelon balls. Serve with French or favorite fruit dressing.

California Products

Every month is vegetable-growing month in California, and the bountiful harvest includes artichokes, asparagus, broccoli, cabbage, carrots, cauliflower, celery, corn, lettuce, onions, peppers of an infinite variety, pumpkin, squash, tomatoes, and the melon family which embraces cantaloupes, crenshaw, casaba, persian and honeydews.

Though California soil is particularly adaptable for bean-growing, farmers concentrate their attention on raising eight popular varieties: baby lima, blackeye, dark red kidney, garbanzo, large lima, light red kidney, pink, and small white. Two of these merit special attention--the garbanzo (chick pea), with its appealing nut-like flavor, mixes well with other salad vegetables, and the pink bean, a staple of the Mexican-American dishes, of barbecue beans, and of chili con carne. When beans are cooked (or served) with corn, rice or wheat, the protein quality of the beans is enhanced. Since beans swell in volume during soaking and cooking, they provide economical protein food.

Prime agricultural land in the Sacramento and San Joaquin valleys is devoted to rice production each year. California rice is planted during April and May by airplanes broadcasting rice seed into flooded fields. The young rice plants develop during the warm summer months and begin to mature by early September. Within a month, the rice has fully matured and ripened to a golden color. Rice byproducts include bran, oil, breakfast cereal kernels, polish, and hulls.

Bees were uncommon in early California, but thanks to the vast cultivated acreage, bees were kept busy in their pursuit of nectar, roaming from desert flowers to citrus groves, producing a natural, unrefined sweet that supplies quick energy. As a sugar substitute, honey may be used in salad dressings, sweet and sour dishes, fruited meats, glazes, breads, cakes, cookies, muffins, icings, jams and a satisfying spread for bread. Since honey can absorb moisture, it should never be refrigerated, but stored in a dry place. If honey should granulate, stand the honey container in a pan of hot (not boiling) water, until it begins to liquefy.

Efficient methods of operation have boosted California's production of turkey to the second highest in the nation; turkey farms dot the landscape in the Sacramento and San Joaquin valley.

The ancient tradition of sheepherding is carried on in Mendocino County, along California's north coast, where lively lambs graze in a pastoral setting.

Lamb

LEG OF LAMB Mendocino County Style

1 LEG OF LAMB (boned)
1 can PINEAPPLE–GRAPEFRUIT JUICE (frozen concentrate, mixed with 1½ cups water)
2 grated APPLES
½ cup BREAD CRUMBS
½ teaspoon ROSEMARY (crushed)
1 teaspoon MINT (crushed)
2 tablespoons BUTTER

marinade

½ of JUICE MIXTURE
1 cup of WINE
1 tablespoon OIL

Salt meat inside. Combine 1/2 juice mixture with apples, crumbs, spices, and butter. Spread mixture over meat. Roll into shape and tie with twine. Combine ingredients for marinade and shake well. Pour marinade into roasting pan and set meat in pan. Let stand overnight in refrigerator, turning occasionally. Drain. Place meat on rack in roasting pan and roast at 450 F for 15 minutes; then at 325 F. Baste frequently til tender (about two hours). Skim off fat and thicken pan juices.

LAMB SHOULDER CUSHION ROAST (with Stuffing)

3 to 4 lb. square cut SHOULDER OF LAMB
2 tablespoons chopped ONION
½ cup chopped CELERY
2 tablespoons BUTTER
1 teaspoon SALT
¼ teaspoon GINGER
2 tablespoons BROWN SUGAR
1 tablespoon DRIED MINT (or fresh mint)
2½ cups chopped APPLES (unpeeled)
1 cup BREAD (Cubed)
¼ cup MILK

Have bones removed from roast to form a pocket. Saute onion and celery in butter. Add remaining ingredients and toss together lightly. Fill lamb cavity with stuffing, sew or skewer edges together. Place fat side up on rack in shallow, uncovered pan. Roast in a 325 F oven about 2 1/2 hours (or til done).

LAMB CHOPS TERIYAKI

6 SHOULDER CHOPS (¾ inch thick)
3 tablespoons SOY SAUCE
1 teaspoon ground GINGER
½ to 1 teaspoon GARLIC SALT
1/8 teaspoon PEPPER
2 teaspoons SUGAR
½ cup ORANGE JUICE
2 ORANGES (cut into 6 wedges)

Arrange chops in flat baking dish. Combine ingredients and pour over. Refrigerate one to two hours. Cover and bake at 350 F an hour (or til tender). Add orange wedges and cover. Skim fat from drippings, thicken with one tablespoon corn starch per cup. Spoon over meat and garnish with orange wedges.

BARBECUED LAMB RIB (with Sauce)

1 cup CATSUP
½ cup SOY SAUCE
1 cup BROWN SUGAR
1 teaspoon GARLIC SALT
2 slices ONION
2 slices LEMON
½ cup fresh PARSLEY (chopped)
3 to 4 lbs. RIB STRIPS

Combine all ingredients except ribs and simmer one hour. Salt and pepper the ribs and place on grill, turning often. Baste with sauce frequently.

LAMB BARBECUE SAUCE

½ cup COOKING OIL
2 tablespoons SOY SAUCE
2 tablespoons WORCESTERSHIRE
1 tablespoon ROSEMARY
2 cloves GARLIC (crushed)
or 1 teaspoon GARLIC POWDER
SALT and PEPPER

Mix ingredients together and brush on roast or any cut of lamb for barbecuing.

SPICED LAMB TONGUES

6 LAMB TONGUES
1 medium sized ONION (quartered)
1 large CARROT (cut up)
2 or 3 sprigs PARSLEY
1 stalk CELERY
1 BAY LEAF
1 tablespoon VINEGAR
3 or 4 PEPPER CORNS
(or whole peppers)

Soak tongues in cold water at least an hour. Drain and wash again in fresh water. Put tongues into pot to boil with the vegetables, seasoning, and cold water to cover. Cover pan and cook til tender (about 1 to 1 1/2 hours). Remove from broth, dip immediately into cold water (to remove skin). Return to broth and serve either hot or cold.

LAMB CHOPS in WINE

6 shoulder LAMB CHOPS
GARLIC, SALT & PEPPER
3 tablespoons BUTTER
1 tablespoon BUTTER
1 ONION (chopped)
2 tablespoons SHALLOTS (chopped)
1 tablespoon PARSLEY (chopped)
1½ tablespoons FLOUR
1 cup DRY WHITE WINE

Rub chops with garlic salt and pepper. Brown on both sides in butter. Transfer chops to a casserole and keep hot. Saute onion, shallots and parsley in tablespoon butter. When these are soft, stir in flour, blending well. Gradually add wine and cook til sauce is thickened, stirring constantly. Pour sauce over lamb chops. Cover casserole with buttered paper and bake in 350 F oven 20 minutes (or til tender). Remove paper from casserole and bake ten minutes longer.

OVEN STEW (Sheepherder's Stew)

1½ to 2 lb. cubed LAMB SHOULDER MEAT
½ cup sliced ONION
4 to 6 sliced CARROTS
½ CABBAGE (sliced rather thickly)
1 can TOMATO SAUCE
4 POTATOES (thickly sliced)
4 cups WATER
1 teaspoon SALT
½ teaspoon PEPPER
½ teaspoon ALLSPICE
1 teaspoon chopped (fresh or dried) ROSEMARY (or thyme)

Set oven at 375 F. Place all ingredients in a large casserole by arranging in layers. Top with water, sauce and spices. Cover tightly with lid or foil and bake for two hours.

ORIENTAL LAMB CHOPS

1 cup dried APRICOTS
1 cup DRIED PRUNES
1 cup WALNUTS
¼ cup NAVY BEANS
2 tablespoons BUTTER
1 cup WATER
½ LIME (sliced)
1 tablespoon CURRY POWDER
12 LAMB CHOPS (shoulder cut may be used)

Soak apricots and prunes for a while. Soak walnuts and beans separately several hours or overnight. Brown meat in butter. Add water and let stew for 15 minutes. Add tenderized fruits, nuts and beans and simmer on low heat for two hours. During last hour of cooking add curry powder and the lime.

ARMENIAN LAMB

4 lbs. SHOULDER OF LAMB
2 ONIONS
2 EGGPLANTS
4 GREEN PEPPERS
4 TOMATOES
SALT and PEPPER
1 cup SHERRY WINE
FOIL

Cut lamb into 8 large pieces and cut each onion and eggplant into 4 pieces. Cut peppers and tomatoes in half. Take 8 pieces of foil and arrange lamb, onion, eggplant, pepper and tomato pieces on each. Sprinkle with salt and pepper, pour two tablespoons of wine over top and wrap tightly. Place foil bundles in roasting pan. Bake in 350 F oven 2 1/2 hours. (Do not turn packages or cover pan.) To serve, unwrap packages.

DEVILED LAMB NECK

1½ lbs. NECK SLICES (¾ thick)
1 cup sliced ONIONS
2 tablespoons OIL (or fat)
2 teaspoons SALT
1 tablespoon VINEGAR
½ teaspoon DRY MUSTARD
1 tablespoon PARSLEY (minced)
2 cups WATER (or 1 cup dry white wine)

Cook lamb and onions in hot fat about 20 minutes. Add rest of ingredients and simmer 1 1/2 hours (or til tender).

SAVORY LAMB PATTIES

2 cups soft BREAD CRUMBS
¼ cup WATER
1½ teaspoons SALT
½ teaspoon PEPPER
2 tablespoons chopped ONION
1 small clove GARLIC (minced)
3 tablespoons minced PARSLEY
1 EGG
1 tablespoon soft BUTTER
1 lb. ground raw LAMB
3 tablespoons FAT

Soak bread crumbs in water. Add egg, lamb, butter, salt, pepper, onion, garlic and parsley. Shape lightly into 8 patties. Dip in flour and simmer 15 minutes in hot fat. Turn to brown.

LAMB SHANKS CHABLIS

4 LAMB SHANKS
Slivers of GARLIC
1 tablespoon OIL
SALT and PEPPER
1 medium ONION (chopped)
1 cup CHABLIS (or dry sauterne)
WATER

Insert sliver of garlic near bone in meaty part of shanks. Brown on all sides in oil in large pot. Season with salt and pepper during cooking. When browned, add onion and wine. Cover and simmer slowly 1 1/2 hours (or til meat is tender). Make gravy by adding water and wine mixed half and half. Serve shanks on platter with vegetables; serve gravy separately.

ROLLED LAMB FLANKS

4 or 5 LAMB FLANKS
SALT and PEPPER
SAGE
ONION (chopped)

Wash and drain flanks well. Arrange on meat board to roll. Salt and pepper, and sprinkle sage according to taste. Cover with chopped onion and roll (tie with string by wrapping the string in half hitches and once lengthwise.) Cover with salted water and boil til tender. Lift from water and drain. Place in 8x10 glass baking dish and set a flat object on top of rolled flanks. Set a heavier weight on top of that. Keep in refrigerator and slice when cold.

ROLLED SAUSAGE Norwegian Style

Place thin strips of salt pork on flank of mutton. Sprinkle with minced onion, salt, pepper and allspice. Roll up like a jelly roll. Sew with a string and tie tightly to hold in filling. Place in pot with sliced onion, celery tops, crushed bay leaves and boiling water to cover. Simmer til meat is tender (about 2 hours). Remove from water. Place in loaf pan and cover with clean cloth. Press the meat by placing a heavy weight on it til cold. (For pressing, place a brick or flatiron in another loaf pan and set on top of cloth-covered meat.) Store in cool place and serve cold, in slices.

HANGTOWN STEAK 'n OYSTER LOAF

1 large loaf FRENCH BREAD
2 teaspoons SALT
¼ teaspoon PEPPER
1 beef FLANK STEAK
1 clove GARLIC (crushed)
½ cup FLOUR
2 EGGS (beaten)
8 large Pacific OYSTERS
¼ lb. BUTTER
3 tablespoons LEMON JUICE
6 drops HOT PEPPER SAUCE

Split loaf in half and pull out as much of the bread as you can, leaving crust intact. Rub the bread through a coarse grater to make 3 cups crumbs. Season with salt and pepper. Rub flank steak with garlic. Slice with sharp knife diagonally across grain into thin strips. Dip beef in flour, then in egg and finally in crumbs. Drain oysters on paper towels and follow same procedure. Melt butter in large skillet and brown steak and oysters on both sides. Arrange on bottom of bread shell. Add lemon juice and pepper sauce to butter in skillet and pour over beef and oysters. Replace top bread shell. Wrap in foil and bake in 375 F oven 15 minutes. (Serves 6)

BEEF SHORT RIBS, California Style

4 lean BEEF SHORT RIBS
1 tablespoon BUTTER
1 medium size ONION (chopped)
1 cup chopped CELERY
1 teaspoon SALT
1/8 teaspoon PEPPER
4 medium sized CARROTS (thinly sliced)
½ teaspoon THYME
1/8 teaspoon SAGE

Trim fat from ribs. Brown beef in butter in heavy skillet or Dutch oven. While browning, add half of onion, celery, salt and pepper. When brown, cover beef with remaining vegetables. Sprinkle with remaining salt and pepper and crumbled thyme and sage. Cover tightly. Bake in 275 F oven 3 hours, til tender.

BEEF BRISKET PAPRIKA

4 to 5 lbs. lean BEEF BRISKET
4 medium ONIONS
1 tablespoon PAPRIKA
2 teaspoons SALT
2 teaspoons minced GARLIC
½ teaspoon PEPPER
½ cup WATER (broth or wine)

Trim off outside fat from beef brisket. Grate enough onion, catching juice, to get a measure of 1/3 cup. Slice remaining onions. Make a paste with grated onion, paprika, salt, minced garlic and pepper. Put brisket flat in broiler or baking pan. Spread with half of paprika paste. Roast in 500 F oven 15 minutes. Turn beef, spread with remaining paprika paste and return to 500 F oven 15 minutes longer. Cover beef with onion slices. Add water, cover pan tightly with foil. Return to oven and reset temperature control to 325 F. Bake 2 1/2 hours longer.

WHEAT GERM BEEF ROLL

1 beef FLANK STEAK (1½ lbs.)
1 tablespoon PREPARED MUSTARD
¾ cup chopped ONION
1/3 cup BUTTER
¾ cup Kretschmer toasted WHEAT GERM
1/3 cup minced PARSLEY
2 tablespoons WORCESTERSHIRE SAUCE
¾ teaspoon THYME (crumbled)
½ teaspoon SALT
¼ teaspoon PEPPER

Starting at one long side, butterfly steak by slicing horizontally to within 1/2-inch of opposite side of steak. Open steak and spread cut surface with mustard. Saute onion lightly in butter. Combine with wheat germ and remaining ingredients. Sprinkle mixture evenly over mustard coated steak. Roll up, starting at long edge. Tie beef roll tightly in several places with string. Place in foil-lined 13x9x2 baking pan. Bake in 375 F oven 45 minutes. Remove from oven, cool, wrap in foil. Refrigerate several hours or overnight. Slice diagonally to serve.

BEEF STEAK SALSA FRIA

4 boneless RIB STEAKS
1 cup chopped TOMATOES
½ cup coarsely chopped ONIONS
1 (4 oz.) can GREEN CHILIS (chopped)
1 tablespoon OLIVE OIL
1 tablespoon VINEGAR
1 teaspoon ground CORIANDER
¼ teaspoon SALT
¼ teaspoon PEPPER

Trim most of outside fat from steak. Keep refrigerated til time to barbecue. Combine all remaining ingredients (makes 2 cups). Chill and serve very cold with hot barbecued steaks. (In cooking steaks over charcoal, build fire about half an hour before cooking time. Coals should be covered with gray ash.)

SPICY YOGURT BEEF KABOBS

2 lbs. boneless BEEF CHUCK (1½ inch chunks)
1½ cups plain YOGURT
¾ cup chopped ONION
1 teaspoon minced GARLIC
1 small dried HOT CHILI PEPPER (chopped)
¾ teaspoon ground CUMIN SEED
½ teaspoon NUTMEG
¼ teaspoon SALT
¼ teaspoon CINNAMON

Toss beef chunks with all remaining ingredients. Cover and refrigerate overnight. String beef on skewers. Barbecue over hot coals about 15 minutes, turning every 5 minutes. (Serves 4)

SWEET 'n SOUR BEEF

2 lb. lean BEEF (cubed)
2 large cans TOMATO SAUCE
1 can WATER
JUICE of 2 LEMONS
1 cup SUGAR
SALT and PEPPER

Brown meat quickly in frypan. Mix tomato sauce, water and lemon juice together and pour over meat. Transfer to baking dish and bake in a 325 F oven for three hours (or til tender)

Turkey

TURKEY DRUMSTICK DINNER

4 TURKEY DRUMSTICKS
2 tablespoons OIL
1 tablespoon BUTTER
1 medium ONION (sliced)
1 can (16 oz.) STEWED TOMATOES
3 CHICKEN BOUILLON CUBES
½ teaspoon SALT
½ teaspoon GARLIC SALT
½ teaspoon OREGANO
½ teaspoon BASIL LEAVES (crumbled)
8 small or 4 large POTATOES
2 or 3 ZUCCHINI (sliced ¾ inch thick)
1 tablespoon CORNSTARCH
2 tablespoons warm WATER

Brown drumsticks on all sides in oil and butter in skillet. Remove to large baking pan and top with onion slices. In same skillet heat tomatoes with chicken base and seasonings. Pour over drumsticks. Cover pan with foil, crimping to edge of pan. Bake about two hours in a 325 F oven til almost tender, basting once or twice. Meanwhile, boil potatoes, slip off skins. Tuck potatoes and zucchini in and around meat and spoon liquid over them. Cover, bake 30 minutes longer. Mix cornstarch and water and stir into hot sauce. Bake 5 to 10 minutes to thicken slightly. Arrange turkey and vegetables on hot platter.

OVEN-BARBECUED TURKEY WINGS

4 TURKEY WINGS
1 teaspoon SALT
2 tablespoons OIL
1 (15 oz.) can TOMATO SAUCE
¼ cup VINEGAR
1 teaspoon CHILI POWDER
¼ teaspoon PEPPER
1/8 teaspoon GARLIC POWDER
1 (8 oz.) can PINEAPPLE SLICES

Sprinkle wings with salt. Brown slowly on all sides in heated oil. Pour off any fat in pan. Combine tomato sauce, vinegar, chili powder, pepper, garlic powder and 1/4 cup syrup drained from pineapple slices. Pour over browned wings, and heat to boiling. Cover pan. Bake in a 350 F oven for 1 1/4 hours, basting once or twice. Uncover, skim off any fat on sauce. Top each wing with pineapple slice. Bake, uncovered, for 15 more minutes.

ORANGE-SAUCED DRUMSTICKS

2½ lbs. TURKEY LEGS
¼ cup FLOUR
½ teaspoon PAPRIKA
¼ teaspoon PEPPER
1 teaspoon SALT
1 teaspoon ground GINGER
2 stalks CELERY (cut up)
1 ONION (sliced)
1 tablespoon BUTTER
1½ cups ORANGE JUICE
3 tablespoons SHERRY

Combine flour and seasonings in paper bag and coat turkey legs. Put celery and sliced onions in greased casserole and top with legs, dotted with butter. Combine juice and sherry, and pour over casserole. Cover and bake in a 350 F oven for 2 1/2 hours til tender. Serve extra sauce over biscuits or rice.

SHERRIED TURKEY

4 TURKEY WINGS (about 2½ lbs.)
SALT and PEPPER
4 tablespoons BUTTER
½ cup SHERRY
1 can (4 oz.) button MUSHROOMS
1 pkg. (1½ oz.) CHICKEN GRAVY MIX
1 cup dairy SOUR CREAM

Lightly sprinkle turkey pieces with salt and pepper. Brown in butter in dutch oven or skillet with cover. Add sherry and liquid from mushrooms. Cover. Bake in 350 F oven for 1 to 1 1/2 hours or til turkey is tender. Remove turkey to serving dish and keep warm. Measure juice in pan and add enough water, if necessary, to make 1 1/4 cups liquid. Carefully blend liquid and gravy mix in dutch oven or skillet. Simmer, uncovered, 5 minutes, stirring continually. Blend in sour cream and mushrooms. When sauce is smooth and hot, pour over turkey. Serve with rice.

TENDER TURKEY THIGHS

4 TURKEY THIGHS
2 tablespoons OIL
1 tablespoon BUTTER
1 (10¾ oz.) can condensed CHICKEN BROTH
1 cup chopped fresh MUSHROOMS
3 tablespoons instant MINCED ONION
½ cup WHITE WINE
1½ teaspoons SALT
1 teaspoon DRY MUSTARD
1 teaspoon PAPRIKA
¼ teaspoon BASIL
¼ teaspoon SAGE
1/8 teaspoon PEPPER
3 tablespoons CORNSTARCH
3 tablespoons WATER

Brown turkey thighs in heavy skillet in oil and butter. Combine all ingredients (except cornstarch and water). Pour over turkey and heat to boiling. Lower heat, cover, and simmer for 1 3/4 hours (or til meat is tender). Remove turkey to serving dish and keep hot. Skim fat from cooking liquid. Mix cornstarch with water and stir into liquid in pan. Cook, stirring, til sauce boils and thickens. Serve over turkey.

TURKEY LOAF

2 lbs. fresh ground TURKEY
3 slices day-old BREAD (pulled into crumbs)
2 EGGS (slightly beaten)
1 medium ONION (minced)
¼ cup minced GREEN PEPPER (optional)
2 tablespoons HORSERADISH
2 teaspoons SALT
1 teaspoon DRY MUSTARD
¼ cup EVAPORATED MILK
¾ cup CATSUP

Lightly mix all ingredients EXCEPT 1/2 cup of catsup. Mold in 9x5x3 loaf pan. Spread top with remaining catsup. Bake in a 375 F oven for 1 1/4 hours. Pour juices from pan. Unmold loaf onto heated platter. (If desired, make gravy from pan juices)

Egg Treats

BASIC OMELET

4 EGGS
¼ cup WATER
½ teaspoon SALT
Dash PEPPER
1 tablespoon BUTTER

Mix eggs, water, salt and pepper with fork. Heat butter in 10-inch omelet pan or skillet til just hot enough to sizzle a drop of water. Pour in egg mixture. Mixture should set at edges at once. With pancake turner, carefully draw cooked portions at edges toward center, so uncooked portions flow to bottom. Tilt skillet to hasten flow of uncooked eggs. Slide pan rapidly back and forth over heat to keep mixture in motion and moving freely in pan. Fill with individual filling, OR while top of omelet is still moist and creamy-looking, fold in half with pancake turner, and flip onto platter. (Serves 2)

HUEVOS RANCHEROS

4 CORN TORTILLAS
8 fresh EGGS (poached)
1 can GREEN CHILI SAUCE (salsa verde)
¼ lb. grated CHEESE

Deep fry tortillas and drain on paper towels. While tortillas are frying, poach eggs. Set two poached eggs on each heated tortilla, top with heated green chili sauce. Sprinkle with grated cheese. Place under broiler a few minutes til cheese is melted.

JACK CHEESE OMELET

1 cup diced Monterey Jack CHEESE
4 slices BACON (cooked and crumbled)
4 EGGS
½ teaspoon SALT
¼ teaspoon PEPPER
Pinch BASIL
Pinch OREGANO
2 tablespoons MILK
2 teaspoons BUTTER

Mix cheese and crumbled bacon. Combine eggs, salt, pepper, basil, oregano and milk. Beat with fork to blend. Heat one teaspoon butter in 6-inch skillet. Pour in half of egg mixture. Cook over medium heat, lifting edge of omelet to let uncooked egg run down into pan. When top is softly set, sprinkle with 1/4 of cheese mixture. Fold omelet over filling and roll carefully out of pan onto ovenproof plate. Sprinkle with 1/4 cheese mixture. (Makes one omelet) Make second omelet in same way. Put both omelets in 400 F oven 5 minutes (or til cheese melts.)

SHIRRED EGGS

Butter six custard cups. Put one tablespoon milk (or cream) into each cup. Break an egg into each and season with salt and pepper. Set cups in a shallow pan. Pour hot water in pan to one-inch depth around cups. Bake at 325 F for 15 minutes (or til eggs are firm). Top with dash of paprika and serve.

MONTEREY FONDUE

12 slices WHITE BREAD
Soft BUTTER
1 can (12 oz.) whole kernel CORN (drained)
1 can (7 oz.) GREEN CHILES
2 cups (½ lb.) grated Monterey JACK CHEESE
4 EGGS (slightly beaten)
3 cups MILK
1 teaspoon SALT

Spread bread with butter (trim crusts, if desired). Cut each slice in half. Arrange half the slices in a buttered 3-quart baking dish (9x13x2). Cover with half the corn. Cut chiles into strips and remove seeds. Arrange half the strips over corn and sprinkle with half the grated cheese. Repeat layers. Combine eggs with milk and salt. Pour over ingredients in casserole. Cover and refrigerate 4 to 5 hours. Bake in 350 F oven 45 minutes (or til golden brown and puffy).

SPICED PUNCH

¼ cup SUGAR
½ teaspoon CINNAMON
¼ teaspoon GINGER
6 EGGS
1 qt. chilled ORANGE JUICE
1 qt. chilled PINEAPPLE JUICE
1 qt. chilled GINGER ALE
ORANGE SHERBET (optional)

Mix sugar and spices. Add eggs; beat well. Stir in chilled juices and ginger ale, blending thoroughly. Add scoops of sherbet, if desired. (Makes about two dozen 1-cup servings)

BASIC CREPE

6 tablespoons BUTTER
6 EGGS (slightly beaten)
1 cup MILK
1 cup WATER
1½ cups all purpose FLOUR
½ teaspoon SALT

Melt butter in 10-inch omelet pan (or 8-inch crepe pan). Pour melted butter into mixing bowl; add eggs, milk, and water and beat together with rotary beater. Blend in flour and salt til mixture is smooth. Heat buttered omelet pan til just hot enough to sizzle a drop of water. For each crepe, pour scant 1/4 cup batter in pan (rotating pan as batter is poured). Cook til lightly browned on bottom; remove from pan or turn and brown other side. (Crepes should set to a thin, lacy pancake almost immediately. If too much batter is poured into pan, pour off excess immediately.) Stack between sheets of paper toweling or waxed paper til ready to use. (Crepes may be frozen.) Spread filling on each crepe; roll up, and serve 3 crepes per person. (Makes about 20 crepes)

Crepe Filling

2 cans (13½ oz. each) PINEAPPLE TIDBITS (well drained)
3 cups MANDARIN ORANGES
1 cup flaked COCONUT
1 cup SOUR CREAM

Combine all ingredients. Chill to blend flavors. Serve on crepes.

COTTAGE CHEESE PANCAKES

6 EGGS (well beaten)
2 cups (1 lb.) small curd creamed COTTAGE CHEESE
½ cup all purpose FLOUR
2 tablespoons BUTTER (melted)
1 teaspoon SALT

Blend together all ingredients til smooth. For each pancake pour approximately 1/4 cup batter onto hot, well-greased griddle. Spread to about 5-inch diameter. Cook til pancake surface is no longer moist in center before turning. Turn and cook other side. (Makes approximately 14 pancakes.)

Orange Pancake Sauce

¼ cup BUTTER (melted)
2 EGGS (slightly beaten)
2 tablespoons grated ORANGE PEEL
1/3 cup ORANGE JUICE
¼ cup SUGAR
1 tablespoon grated LEMON PEEL
2 tablespoons LEMON JUICE
CONFECTIONER'S SUGAR
ORANGE SLICES (optional)

Combine all ingredients except confectioner's sugar and orange slices in small saucepan. Mix well. Cook over medium heat, stirring constantly til smooth and thickened. (Makes 1 cup sauce)

BOREGO SPRINGS BUTTERMILK BREAD

1½ cups BUTTERMILK
1 EGG
3 cups BISCUIT MIX
2 tablespoons SUGAR
1 cup (¼ lb.) grated SWISS CHEESE
1 cup sliced pimiento STUFFED OLIVES (drained)
¾ cup chopped WALNUTS

Combine buttermilk, egg, biscuit mix and sugar; beat one minute to blend thoroughly. Gently stir in cheese, olives and walnuts. Spoon into well-buttered pan 9x5x3. Bake in 350 F oven 50 to 55 minutes. (A crack should appear on top of loaf). Cool five minutes before removing from pan. Continue cooling on wire rack. Wrap unused portion; store in refrigerator or freezer.

BAKED CROQUETTES CALIFORNIAN

2/3 cup SOUR CREAM
2 teaspoons WORCESTERSHIRE
1 teaspoon instant minced ONION
½ teaspoon MARJORAM
1 tablespoon LEMON JUICE
½ teaspoon SALT
¼ teaspoon PEPPER
3 cups cooked regular WHITE RICE (or 1 cup raw)
2 cups flaked SALMON (1 lb. can, drained)
½ cup CORN FLAKE CRUMBS

Combine sour cream with seasonings. Add rice and salmon. Chill several hours. Use about 1/3 cup of the chilled mixture at a time to form egg shapes or cone-shaped croquettes. Roll in crumbs. Place in shallow buttered baking dish and bake in 450 F oven 20 minutes (or til lightly browned).

SAN FRANCISCO FRIED CREAM

¼ cup SUGAR
¼ teaspoon SALT
4 tablespoons CORNSTARCH
3 EGG YOLKS
½ pint WHIPPING CREAM
1 teaspoon VANILLA
BRANDY
Finely ground ALMONDS
2 EGGS (beaten)
Fine dry BREAD CRUMBS
SALAD OIL

Combine sugar, salt, cornstarch and egg yolks with whipping cream. Cook over hot water, stirring til thick. Remove from heat. Stir in vanilla and 1 tablespoon brandy. Pour into shallow buttered pan so custard is about 3/4-inch thick. Chill several hours. Cut into squares or rectangles. Coat with almonds, roll in beaten eggs and coat with crumbs. (Fried cream may be prepared this far and then refrigerated.) Shortly before serving, heat oil to 375 and fry crumb-coated cream til golden. Top with warm brandy, ignite and serve flaming. (Serves 6)

SOUR CREAM PEACH PIE

½ cup (1 stick) soft BUTTER
1 (3 oz. pkg.) CREAM CHEESE
¼ teaspoon SALT
1 cup sifted FLOUR
1 No. 2½ can (1 lb. 13 oz.) sliced CLING PEACHES (well drained)
1 cup (½ pint) SOUR CREAM
1 large EGG (slightly beaten)
¼ cup CONFECTIONER'S SUGAR
½ teaspoon pure VANILLA EXTRACT
CINNAMON (or nutmeg)

Cream butter and cheese with salt. Work flour into butter mixture with pastry blender til well blended. Form into ball and roll out on floured board to fit 9-inch pie plate. Pat firmly into pie plate and flute edges to inside rim only. Spread lightly with thin coating of butter. Dry peach slices between paper towels and arrange in circular overlapping pattern in bottom of pastry. Combine sour cream with egg, sugar, and vanilla. Spoon over peaches. Sprinkle with cinnamon or nutmeg. Bake in 425 F oven for 12 minutes. Reduce heat to 350 F and bake 15 to 20 minutes more. Serve warm or cold.

OLD-FASHIONED EGGNOG

6 EGGS (slightly beaten)
4 cups MILK
¼ cup SUGAR
2 teaspoons BRANDY EXTRACT or RUM EXTRACT (or ¾ to 1 cup brandy or rum)
¼ teaspoon SALT
2 cups WHIPPED CREAM (or 1 pint vanilla ice cream)
NUTMEG (optional)

Mix eggs, milk, sugar, extract and salt til well blended. Fold in whipped cream. Pour into bowl or pitcher; cover and refrigerate several hours or overnight. Sprinkle each serving with nutmeg, if desired. (Makes seven 1-cup servings.)

CREAM CHEESE PIE

2 cups GRAHAM CRACKER CRUMBS (about 14 double crackers)
½ cup BUTTER (melted)
½ cup fresh LEMON JUICE
½ pint Whipping CREAM
1 (8 oz.) pkg. CREAM CHEESE
1 can CONDENSED MILK (not evaporated)
1 envelope plain GELATINE
¼ cup cold WATER
1 teaspoon pure VANILLA EXTRACT
1 cup (½ pint) SOUR CREAM (optional)

Use 9-inch deep dish pie plate for crust. Combine crumbs and butter til thoroughly mixed. Line pie plate with 3/4 of the crumb mixture. Stir lemon juice into cream and let stand for 10 minutes. Mash softened cream cheese and beat in condensed milk gradually. Set cheese mixture aside. Add gelatine to water in double boiler top and let stand for five minutes. Dissolve over hot water. Whip lemon-cream mixture til it begins to stiffen. Pour in cream cheese mixture and beat til completely blended. Add dissolved gelatin, stir, and add vanilla. Pour into graham cracker crumb pie crust and chill til firm. Top with sour cream or fresh fruit, if desired. Sprinkle top with remaining cracker crumbs.

JIFFY CUSTARDS

4 EGGS (beaten)
¼ to 1/3 cup SUGAR (or honey)
¼ teaspoon SALT
1 teaspoon Pure VANILLA EXTRACT
2 cups MILK

Combine all ingredients. Cover bottoms of 6 glass (NOT pottery or plastic) custard cups with one of the variations. Pour custard mixture into cups. Place cups on a metal rack in large frying pan. Pour cold water into pan to half the height of custard cups and cover tightly. Bring water to rolling boil. Remove pan from heat. Allow custards to steam in covered pan 12 to 15 minutes (or til knife inserted in center comes out clean). Serve immediately or refrigerate til cold.

Variations

For custard variations, try orange sauce, chopped walnuts, raisins, diced dates, drained fruit cocktail, or chopped nuts.

Orange Sauce for Custard

¼ cup SUGAR
1 tablespoon CORNSTARCH
2/3 cup ORANGE JUICE
1 tablespoon LEMON JUICE
½ teaspoon grated ORANGE PEEL

Combine sugar and cornstarch in saucepan. Combine orange and lemon juices. Gradually pour into sugar mixture, stirring constantly. Bring to boil, stirring constantly. Boil one minute. Remove from heat and stir in peel. Cool slightly before spooning over custard. (Makes about 3/4 cup sauce.)

CANTONESE CHICKEN

2 frying CHICKENS (disjointed)
¼ cup HONEY
¼ cup SOY SAUCE
½ cup CATSUP
¼ cup fresh LEMON JUICE

Arrange chicken pieces in single layer in large baking pan. Mix honey, soy sauce, catsup and lemon juice. Pour over chicken pieces. Allow chicken to stand in marinade several hours (or overnight). Cover pan with foil. Heat oven to 325 F. Bake one hour. Remove foil, baste with sauce. Return to oven and bake uncovered til tender. (If thick sauce is desired, add one tablespoon cornstarch, moistened to smooth paste in cold water.) Serve over cooked rice.

WINE GLAZED HAM

1 center cut ready-to-eat HAM SLICE (about 2 inches thick)
2 teaspoons DRY MUSTARD
1/3 cup HONEY
½ cup PORT or SHERRY

Trim ham slice and score fat. Rub slice with dry mustard, using one teaspoon mustard for each side. Place in a shallow baking pan. Combine honey and wine. Pour over ham. Heat oven to 350 F. Bake uncovered 35 minutes (or til done).

HONEYED POT ROAST

3½ to 4 lb. Chuck, Blade or other POT ROAST
½ pkg. ONION SOUP MIX (2 tablespoons)
3 tablespoons WATER or DRY RED WINE
½ cup TOMATO JUICE
2 tablespoons HONEY
1 BAY LEAF

Place roast in center of wide piece of heavy duty aluminum foil in roasting pan. Bring foil up around sides of roast. Mix together onion soup and wine. Stir in tomato juice and honey. Blend and pour over roast. Add bay leaf. Wrap foil loosely around meat. Seal edges to form an air-tight package. Heat oven to 325 F and bake roast 45 minutes per pound. Skim off fat before thickening meat juices for gravy.

CHICKEN & PEACH BAKE

1 frying CHICKEN (disjointed)
SALT and PEPPER
1 cup CATSUP
½ cup HONEY
1 large LEMON (sliced)
1 can (1 lb. 13 oz.) cling PEACH HALVES

Arrange pieces of chicken in shallow baking pan. Season with salt and pepper. Combine catsup and honey. Pour over chicken, turning pieces to coat all sides. Place slices of lemon over the chicken. Heat oven to 325 F and bake uncovered one hour or til tender. Turn chicken pieces once while baking. During last 15 minutes of baking, increase heat to 350 degrees. Serve on platter with well-drained cling peaches around chicken.

MUFFIN MEAT LOAVES

1 EGG
½ cup MILK
1½ teaspoons SALT
¼ teaspoon PAPRIKA
¼ teaspoon PEPPER
¾ cup BREAD CRUMBS
1 lb. GROUND CHUCK

In a large bowl, beat egg slightly with fork. Add milk, seasonings, bread crumbs and the meat. Blend together lightly. Put one teaspoon of Zesty Sauce in the bottom of six (3-inch) muffin cups. Divide meat mixture evenly into each cup. Shape lightly to resemble muffin. Heat oven to 350 F and bake 25 minutes, or according to personal taste. Serve hot with additional sauce.

Zesty Honey Sauce

1 can (15 oz.) or 2 cans (8 oz. each) TOMATO SAUCE (with tomato bits)
2 tablespoons HONEY
2 tablespoons WINE VINEGAR
1 clove GARLIC (finely minced)
2 green ONIONS (thinly sliced) (tops included)
2 tablespoons diced canned GREEN CHILIES

Combine all ingredients and heat. Use as muffin sauce. May also be used as chilled dip. (Makes 2 cups sauce)

TROPICAL TEA BREAD

1/3 cup soft BUTTER (or margarine)
2/3 cup mild flavored HONEY
2 EGGS
2 tablespoons MILK
½ teaspoon VANILLA
2 cups sifted all purpose FLOUR
½ teaspoon SALT
1 teaspoon BAKING POWDER
½ teaspoon SODA
1 cup flaked COCONUT (toasted)
1 cup mashed ripe BANANAS (2 or 3)
2 teaspoons grated LEMON PEEL
1 teaspoon fresh LEMON JUICE

In large mixing bowl, cream butter. Continue creaming while adding honey in a fine stream. Beat in eggs one at a time. Stir in milk and vanilla. Sift flour with salt, baking powder and soda. Add toasted coconut. Blend together mashed bananas, lemon peel and juice. Add dry ingredients alternately with banana mixture, blending only until all dry ingredients are moistened. Spoon into well greased 9x5x3 pan. Heat oven to 350 F, and bake 55 minutes or til loaf tests done. Cool in pan five minutes. Remove from pan and cool on wire rack. Bread slices thinner if stored overnight or frozen.

HONEY BUTTER

½ cup BUTTER
¼ cup mild flavored HONEY
1 teaspoon CINNAMON

In small mixer bowl, cream butter until fluffy. Continue the creaming process, while adding honey in a thin stream. Store in refrigerator. (For variety, try adding 2 tablespoons fresh lemon or orange juice, and 1 teaspoon grated fruit peel.)

HONEY FUDGE BROWNIES

½ cup BUTTER
2 1-oz. squares UNSWEETENED CHOCOLATE
½ teaspoon SALT
1 teaspoon VANILLA
1 cup HONEY
1/3 cup unsifted all purpose FLOUR
1 teaspoon BAKING POWDER
2 EGGS
1 cup coarsely chopped WALNUTS

In a saucepan, melt together over very low heat: butter, salt, chocolate, and vanilla. Mix well. Remove from heat, blend in honey, flour and baking powder. Add eggs and beat well. Add walnuts. Pour into greased 9x9x2 pan. Heat oven to 325 F. Bake 35 minutes, or til done in center. Cool on rack 15 minutes; mark into squares. (Makes 16)

HONEY DATE LOAF

¼ cup BUTTER
½ cup mild flavored HONEY
1 EGG
2 cups sifted all purpose FLOUR
1 teaspoon SALT
½ teaspoon SODA
1 tablespoon BAKING POWDER
1 can (8¼ oz.) CRUSHED PINEAPPLE
2 teaspoons VANILLA
¾ cup finely snipped, pitted DATES

In large mixing bowl, cream butter until soft. Continue creaming while adding honey in a fine stream. Add egg, beat well. Sift together dry ingredients. Add dry ingredients alternately with pineapple to creamed mixture. Beat until well-blended. Stir in vanilla and dates. Spoon batter into greased 9x5x3 pan and bake at 325 F one hour (or til loaf tests done in center.) Let stand 10 minutes. Remove from pan and cool on wire rack.

HONEY APRICOT LOAF

1 cup HONEY
½ cup boiling WATER
½ cup sliced dried APRICOTS
1 cup pitted DATES (diced)
1 cup chopped WALNUTS
1 EGG
¼ cup SALAD OIL
1 cup MILK
3 cups sifted all-purpose FLOUR
3 teaspoons BAKING POWDER
1 teaspoon SALT
½ teaspoon CINNAMON (or vanilla)

Combine honey, boiling water, apricots and dates. Allow to stand til cool. Add walnuts. In mixing bowl, beat egg slightly. Add oil and milk. Fold in prepared fruit and sifted dry ingredients. Mix only til dry ingredients are blended. Pour batter into oiled, lined 10x5x3 loaf pan. Let stand 15 minutes. Heat oven to 350 F. Bake about 1 1/4 hours (or til loaf tests done in center). Cool in pan five minutes. Remove paper and cool on rack.

MINI CHEESE CAKES

Brown Sugar Crust

½ cup BUTTER
½ cup firmly packed BROWN SUGAR
1¼ cups unsifted all purpose FLOUR

Cream butter and brown sugar thoroughly. Add flour. Blend til mixture resembles fine crumbs. Set aside one cup of mixture. Press remaining mixture into 8-inch square pan, building up sides slightly. Heat oven to 350 F and bake 12 minutes. Cool.

Cream Cheese Filling

1 pkg. (8 oz.) CREAM CHEESE
¼ teaspoon SALT
2 teaspoons FLOUR
¼ cup mild flavored HONEY
1 teaspoon grated LEMON PEEL
1 tablespoon fresh LEMON JUICE
½ teaspoon VANILLA
1 EGG (slightly beaten)
2 tablespoons MILK

Cream cheese with salt, flour and honey til soft. Add grated lemon peel, lemon juice and vanilla. Mix thoroughly. Combine slightly beaten egg and milk. Add to cheese mixture and blend well. Spread mixture over baked crust. Sprinkle and pat the reserved crumbs evenly over top of filling. Bake at 350 F for 30 minutes longer. Cool on rack before cutting into bite-size squares. (Makes 36 squares).

CHOCOLATE CHIP NUT BREAD

¾ cup MILK
½ cup mild flavored HONEY
1 EGG
½ cup fresh ORANGE JUICE
1 pkg. (6 oz.) SEMI-SWEET CHOCOLATE PIECES
3½ cups Buttermilk BISCUIT MIX
1 tablespoon grated ORANGE PEEL
¾ cup finely chopped WALNUTS

In a medium saucepan, warm together milk and honey only until blended. COOL. Stir in egg and orange juice. Add the chocolate pieces. In separate large mixing bowl, measure the biscuit mix. Add milk mixture, stirring only til blended. Do not beat. Add orange peel and nuts. Spoon into greased, lined 9x5x3 pan. Heat oven to 350 F and bake 45 to 55 minutes, or til bread tests done in center. Cool in pan 15 minutes. Remove from pan and cool on wire rack. (Flavor improves and bread slices better if allowed to stand one day before cutting.)

HONEYED STRAWBERRIES

2 cups STRAWBERRIES (hulled)
½ cup HONEY
½ cup fresh ORANGE JUICE (or sweet Sherry Wine)

Place strawberries in colander or strainer. Wash gently in bowl of cold water before hulling and slicing. Combine honey with orange juice or sherry. Pour over berries and chill.

PEPPER STEAK CABALLERO

1½ lbs. SIRLOIN STEAK (strips 1/8 inch thick)
1 tablespoon PAPRIKA
2 cloves GARLIC (crushed)
2 tablespoons BUTTER
1 cup sliced GREEN ONIONS (with tops)
2 GREEN PEPPERS (in strips)
2 large, fresh TOMATOES (diced)
1 cup BEEF BROTH
¼ cup WATER
2 tablespoons CORNSTARCH
2 tablespoons SOY SAUCE
3 cups hot cooked RICE

Sprinkle steak with paprika and allow to stand while preparing other ingredients. Cook steak and garlic in butter til meat is browned. Add onions and green peppers. Continue cooking til vegetables are wilted. Add tomatoes and broth. Cover and simmer about 15 minutes. Blend water with cornstarch and soy sauce. Stir into steak and cook til thickened. Serve on rice.

QUICK PLACER PILAF

2 tablespoons BUTTER
1 cup RICE
1 pkg. DRIED CHICKEN NOODLE SOUP
2 cups boiling WATER

Fry rice in melted butter or margarine until light brown. Sprinkle soup on rice. Add boiling water. Turn heat to low. Cover tightly. Cook rice mixture 20-25 minutes. (Serves 4)

PILAF of SEAFOOD

1 medium sized ONION (chopped)
2 tablespoons SHORTENING
2 cups cooked RICE
2 cups (1 lb. can) TOMATOES
3 stalks CELERY (diced)
½ teaspoon SALT
¼ teaspoon PAPRIKA
½ BAY LEAF (crumbled)
¼ cup grated CHEESE
1 cup cooked SHRIMP (or crabmeat)

Cook onion in shortening til browned. Stir in rice. Combine tomatoes, celery, salt, paprika, bay leaf, and cheese in pan. Heat til cheese is melted. Fold in rice and seafood. Pour into a greased casserole. Cover. Bake in 325 F oven 25 minutes.

LAMB-RICE CASSEROLE

½ LEMON
4 thick LAMB CHOPS
¾ cup BROWN RICE (uncooked)
1 can CONSOMME (10½ oz.)
10 small pearl ONIONS
2 CARROTS (cut in strips)
1 cup SAUTERNE WINE
¼ teaspoon MARJORAM
1/8 teaspoon OREGANO
½ teaspoon SALT
Dash of PEPPER

Squeeze lemon over chops. While this is standing, put in the casserole brown rice, consomme, carrots, onions and sauterne. Add lamb chops. Bake covered 1 hour in 350 F oven. At the end of 1/2 hour, take out and stir, and add seasoning. Return to oven and finish cooking. (Makes 4 servings)

OLD-FASHIONED RICE CUSTARD

6 EGGS
3 cups MILK
1 cup SUGAR
1 teaspoon VANILLA
½ teaspoon SALT
1½ cups cooked RICE
1 cup light RAISINS

Break eggs into a 2-quart buttered casserole; beat slightly with a fork. Add milk, sugar, vanilla, and salt. Blend well. Stir in rice and raisins. Set casserole in pan of water and bake, uncovered, at 350 F for 1 1/4 hours, stirring once after 1/2 hour of baking. (Makes 6 servings)

HONEY RICE

3 cups cooked RICE
½ cup seedless RAISINS
2½ cups MILK
½ cup HONEY
2 tablespoons BUTTER
1 teaspoon grated LEMON PEEL
1 tablespoon LEMON JUICE

Combine rice, raisins, milk, honey, and butter. Bring to a boil, reduce the heat and simmer for 15 minutes, stirring occasionally. Stir in lemon peel and juice.

FRUITED RICE

1 cup sliced CARROTS
3 tablespoons VEGETABLE OIL
1 cup sliced GREEN ONIONS
2 cups APPLES
(sliced, cored unpeeled)
3 cups cooked BROWN RICE
1 teaspoon SALT
½ cup seedless RAISINS
1 tablespoon SESAME SEEDS

Saute carrots in oil about 10 minutes. Add onions and apples. Cook 10 minutes longer. Stir in rice, salt, and raisins. Cook, stirring constantly, til rice is heated. Add sesame seeds.

LEBANESE LENTILS & RICE

1 cup dry LENTILS
1 cup raw RICE
¼ cup BUTTER
4 Calif. PLUMS (chopped)
1 ONION (finely chopped)
1 GREEN APPLE (peeled, chopped)
1½ teaspoons SALT
½ teaspoon CINNAMON

Preheat oven to 350 F. Cook lentils and rice separately as packages direct. Drain lentils and rice well and toss together in large bowl. In skillet, melt butter and cook plums, onion and apple til soft. Add to lentil/rice mixture. Add remaining ingredients and mix well. Spoon into greased 2-quart casserole and cover. Bake 35 to 40 minutes. (Makes 6 servings)

FRIED RICE

1 cup sliced GREEN ONIONS
2 tablespoons VEGETABLE OIL
3 cups cooked BROWN RICE
2 tablespoons SOY SAUCE

Saute green onions in oil til tender. Add rice and cook, stirring constantly, until rice is thoroughly heated. Stir in soy sauce.

FIESTA RICE

5 or 6 slices BACON
½ cup RED ONION (chopped)
½ cup GREEN PEPPER (chopped)
½ cup CELERY (sliced)
1 cup Golden Pearl Calif. RICE
½ teaspoon OREGANO
½ teaspoon SWEET BASIL
1 teaspoon SALT
½ teaspoon PEPPER
1 to 2 teaspoons CHILI POWDER
1 BEEF BOUILLON CUBE
1 can (1 lb.) TOMATOES (drained and cut up, save liquid)
2 teaspoons SOY SAUCE
Boiling WATER
1 teaspoon PARSLEY FLAKES
1 can KIDNEY BEANS (drained)

Fry bacon til crisp, drain, dice and set aside. Saute onions, green pepper and celery in bacon drippings. Add rice and spices and brown together. Dissolve bouillon cube in tomato liquid, soy sauce and enough boiling water to measure 1 1/2 cups. Add liquid, parsley, drained kidney beans and tomatoes to rice mixture. Transfer mixture to buttered casserole. Cover and bake in 350 F oven for 35 minutes. Uncover, fluff with fork, and return to oven, uncovered, an additional 10 minutes. Just before serving, stir in diced bacon.

WESTERN RICE

¾ lb. bulk SAUSAGE
1 hot type SAUSAGE (or 5 slices salami, diced)
¼ cup GREEN PEPPER (chopped)
3 GREEN ONIONS (with tops, chopped)
1 clove GARLIC
1 cup Golden Pearl Calif. RICE
1½ cups BEEF BROTH
½ cup fresh TOMATO (Diced)
3 tablespoons PARSLEY FLAKES
¼ teaspoon MARJORAM
¼ teaspoon SWEET BASIL
¼ teaspoon SAVORY
1 teaspoon SALT
PEPPER to taste

Saute sausage meats, green pepper, onions and garlic. Add rice and brown all for 10 minutes. Add remainder of ingredients (beef broth, tomato, parsley and spices). Pour mixture into covered casserole and bake in 350 F oven for 35 minutes. Remove from oven, fluff with fork and return to oven, uncovered, an additional 10 minutes (or til all liquid is absorbed).

GOLDEN SPANISH RICE

½ cup uncooked RICE
1 cup WATER
1 teaspoon SALT
½ cup chopped ONION
½ cup chopped CELERY
1/3 cup chopped GREEN PEPPER
1 cup stewed TOMATOES
1 teaspoon SUGAR
1 teaspoon CHILI POWDER
½ teaspoon MONOSODIUM GLUTAMATE
½ teaspoon WORCESTERSHIRE SAUCE
1½ tablespoons BUTTER (melted)

Combine rice, water and 1/2 teaspoon salt. Heat to boiling. Stir; cover, and reduce heat. Simmer til rice is tender and liquid absorbed (about 15 minutes). Cook onion, celery, and green pepper in butter til tender. Add remaining ingredients. Stir in cooked rice and simmer til thick. (Makes 4 servings)

BEAN SOAKING

Dry beans can be cooked without soaking, but soaking cuts down cooking time and pot-watching. Try these methods:

ONE-HOUR HOT SOAK: to one pound of California dry beans, any variety, add 6 to 8 cups hot water. Heat to boiling, boil 2 minutes, then set aside for an hour or so before draining and cooking. (This method does in one hour what 15 hours of cold soaking accomplishes.)

OVERNIGHT SALT SOAK: to one pound of California dry beans, add 6 cups cold water and 2 teaspoons salt. Let stand overnight or for several hours. (The salt helps beans to absorb water more evenly, and keep their shape better.)

ANY-BEAN, ANY-BONE SOUP

- 1½ cups small WHITE BEANS
- A MEATY BONE (or bones)
- 2 qts. cold WATER
- 1½ teaspoon SALT (or garlic salt)
- ¼ teaspoon WHITE PEPPER
- ½ a BAY LEAF
- ¼ teaspoon each crumbled THYME and MARJORAM
- 1 cup (or more) chopped ONION
- 1 cup chopped CELERY
- 1 CARROT (chopped)

Put "bone(s)" into large pot, add cold water, heat to boiling, and skim before adding soaked beans, herbs and seasonings. Cover and boil gently two hours or til beans are very tender. Take out bone and remove meat. Cut up meat and add to soup along with vegetables. Cook 30 to 40 minutes longer. Add hot water (or canned broth or canned tomatoes) if desired to thin soup to right consistency. Add salt and pepper to taste.

CALIFORNIA SUNSHINE SALAD

- 2 cups cooked or canned GARBANZOS (drained)
- 1 can (8¾ oz.) golden whole-kernel CORN (drained)
- 1 cup diced (or sliced) CELERY
- ½ cup chopped ONION
- 2 tablespoons diced PIMIENTO
- ¼ cup diced GREEN PEPPER

Combine ingredients and moisten to taste with Golden Gate Salad Dressing. Chill and serve. (Makes one quart)

Golden Gate Salad Dressing

- 1/3 cup SUGAR
- ½ teaspoon DRY MUSTARD
- 1 teaspoon SALT
- 2 tablespoons FLOUR
- 1 EGG (or 2 yolks)
- ½ cup VINEGAR
- ½ cup WATER
- 1 tablespoon BUTTER

Mix dry ingredients. Beat egg with fork in small bowl. Beat in dry mixture. Heat vinegar, water, and butter in saucepan. Remove from heat and gradually add egg mixture, stirring fast. Then put back to cook, stirring constantly 2 or 3 minutes, til smooth and thick. (Makes 1 3/4 cups dressing).

PINK BEANS--PORTUGUESE STYLE

1 lb. Calif. PINK BEANS
1 tablespoon CUMIN SEED
4 slices BACON
1 small ONION
½ GREEN PEPPER
1 clove GARLIC
½ teaspoon CINNAMON
¼ teaspoon PEPPER
1 8-ounce can TOMATO SAUCE
1/3 cup CATSUP

Soak beans overnight. Drain, cover generously with water, bring to boil, then turn heat to simmer. Add cumin seed and simmer for an hour. Meanwhile, cut up bacon and cook in frying pan til clear. Chop onion, pepper and garlic. Add to bacon and cook til soft. Add cinnamon, pepper, tomato sauce, and catsup. Heat to boiling, add to beans, and continue cooking (about 45 minutes, or til tender). Add salt and pepper to taste.

CHILIBEANS

Cover one pound (2 cups) California pink beans (or light red kidney beans) with boiling water and let stand an hour or so. Drain beans, put into a large, heavy pot, cover with boiling water again and add:

1 ONION (chopped) (about ¾ cup)
1 to 3 cloves GARLIC (minced)
1/3 cup BACON DRIPPINGS (or oil)
1½ teaspoon SALT
1 can (8 oz.) TOMATO SAUCE
1½ teaspoon CHILI POWDER
¼ teaspoon CUMIN SEED (or powder)

Cook slowly (covered), about three hours, til beans are tender and a rich sauce is formed. Add more hot water if necessary. Beans should be neither too dry nor too juicy.

These Chilibeans will make 8 to 10 servings as a side dish. To make them into Chili Con Carne for a main dish, cook the following meat sauce separately while beans are simmering:

CHILI CON CARNE SAUCE

2 tablespoons OIL (or bacon drippings)
2 lbs. HAMBURGER (not too lean)
3 or 4 cloves GARLIC (minced)
1 ONION (chopped, about 1 cup)
1 can (8 oz.) TOMATO SAUCE
1½ teaspoon SALT
2 to 3 tablespoons CHILI POWDER
½ teaspoon CUMIN SEED
3 cups hot WATER (plus more as needed)
¼ cup FLOUR

Heat oil. Add hamburger and cook, stirring and turning til meat loses red color. Stir in all other ingredients, cover, and cook slowly about 3 hours (or longer) to a thick, rich consistency. Before adding sauce to beans, add one cup of hot water to the sauce, then thicken slightly, using 1/4 cup flour mixed smooth with 1/3 cup warm water. Stir into beans; add salt if needed.

Vegetables

BASIC BROCCOLI

Wash broccoli and trim a bit off ends of stems, but do not remove branches. If stems are over 1/2 inch in diameter, make lengthwise gashes through them almost to the flowerets. The stalks will then cook as quickly as the flower buds. Drop the broccoli into a small amount of boiling salted water. Cover and cook quickly just til tender, about 10 minutes. Serve hot.

FRIED BROCCOLI

1½ lbs. fresh BROCCOLI
1 teaspoon SALT
Boiling WATER
¼ cup cooking OIL
1 clove GARLIC
2 tablespoons finely minced ONIONS
2 tablespoons LEMON JUICE

Wash broccoli; split each stalk lengthwise just to the flower. Place flat in large skillet; sprinkle with salt; pour in boiling water til 1-inch deep. Cover and simmer 15 minutes (or til stalks are tender-crisp). Lift out to pie plate. Pour water out of skillet; then pour in oil. Add garlic and onion and cook til golden. Discard garlic; add broccoli and heat, shaking gently, til well coated. Add more salt if necessary and drizzle with lemon juice. (Makes 4 servings)

FRENCH FRIED EGGPLANT

Pare eggplant and cut in 1/4 inch slices crosswise. Sprinkle with salt, garlic salt, and pepper. Dip in flour. Then dip in egg which has been beaten with 2 tablespoons of milk. Roll in fine, dry bread crumbs til completely covered. Fry in hot fat (try olive oil) from 2 to 4 minutes. Drain and serve hot.

EGGPLANT a la MEXICO

1 lb. EGGPLANT
½ cup boiling WATER
1 small ONION (chopped)
½ teaspoon SALT
2 cups fresh TOMATOES (chopped)
½ cup ONION (finely chopped)
1 clove GARLIC (minced)
¼ cup diced GREEN CHILIS
½ teaspoon SALT
¼ teaspoon SWEET BASIL
2 EGGS (beaten)
1 cup grated MONTEREY CHEESE

Peel and cut eggplant into 1'' cubes and cook with onion in boiling salted water for 10 minutes. Drain. Combine the rest of ingredients, except cheese. Put into oiled 1 1/2 qt. casserole. Cover and bake in 375 F oven for 1/2 hour. Remove cover and reduce heat to 350 F. Sprinkle top with cheese. Continue to bake til cheese melts and becomes bubbly. (Serves 4)

BASIC ASPARAGUS

Wash asparagus to remove grit, but do not soak stalks. Cut off ends of stalks. Wrap asparagus in aluminum foil and set in skillet. (To speed cooking, prick foil with fork in several places before placing in skillet.) Add cold water to skillet to cover package; cover pan and bring water to boil. Cook about ten minutes (or til tender).

ASPARAGUS PIE

- ¼ cup BUTTER
- ¼ cup FLOUR
- ¾ cup CHICKEN BROTH
- ¾ cup MILK
- ½ cup grated CHEDDAR CHEESE
- ¼ cup grated PARMESAN CHEESE
- ½ teaspoon SALT
- 1/8 teaspoon PEPPER
- 2 lbs. hot, freshly cooked ASPARAGUS SPEARS
- 2 tablespoons grated PARMESAN CHEESE

Melt butter and blend in flour. Add broth and milk and cook, stirring constantly, til mixture is thick and bubbling. Add cheeses and seasonings. Stir til cheeses melt. Set asparagus spears in pie tin. Pour sauce over spears and sprinkle with cheese. Broil several minutes til browned and bubbly.

BASIC ARTICHOKES

Wash artichokes. Cut 1'' off, straight across top. Pull off loose leaves at bottom. Clip off spine tips with scissors. Drop artichokes into pot of boiling salted water to which olive oil, garlic, bay leaf, and fresh lemon slices have been added. Cover tightly and boil 20 to 40 minutes (til leaf can be pulled easily from base). Drain upside down. Remove choke (thistle portion) with spoon from center of artichoke. Serve as hot vegetable with hot melted butter or hollandaise sauce. To serve cold, chill cooked artichoke, set upright on plate and serve with fresh lemon juice and favorite dip. To eat: pull off petals one by one and dip base into sauce. Eat only tender base part of leaf by drawing it between teeth. Discard remaining tip. Artichoke bottom is good to eat, too.

COLD ARTICHOKE with SEAFOOD

Boil artichokes, cool, and chill in refrigerator. At serving time, prepare artichokes for stuffing by gently pushing leaves outward. Fill with seafood salad and serve with dressing.

- 2 cups cooked SHRIMP (chilled)
- 1 cup sliced CELERY
- 2 tablespoon fresh LEMON JUICE
- ½ cup MAYONNAISE
- SALT and PEPPER to taste

Cut shrimps into halves lengthwise and mix with remaining ingredients. Chill several hours before stuffing.

SKILLET TOMATOES

¼ cup BUTTER
½ cup finely chopped ONION
2 tablespoons chopped PARSLEY
½ teaspoon SALT
¼ teaspoon THYME LEAVES
1/8 teaspoon PEPPER
6 whole TOMATOES (peeled and cored)

Melt butter in skillet. Add onion, parsley, salt, thyme and pepper. Place tomatoes (core side down) on top, and cover. Cook 5 minutes, then turn tomatoes, basting with mixture. Cover and cook an additional 5 minutes. Serve as side dish.

ALL-DAY BEANS 'n TOMATOES

1 lb. PINK BEANS
1 large ONION
1 (No. 2½ can) ground PLUM TOMATOES
2 (No. 303 cans) Stewed TOMATOES
1 (No. 300 can) BEEF CONSOMME (or homemade stock)
1 cup RED WINE (and a touch of Brandy)
1 to 2 lbs. lean GROUND BEEF
SALT and PEPPER
CHILI PEPPERS (optional)

Wash and soak beans overnight. Next morning, simmer about one hour. In iron skillet, brown the sliced onion lightly. Add onion to tomatoes, consomme and wine. Add to cooked beans. In the same skillet, brown the meat lightly, breaking up and turning frequently. Salt and pepper meat and add to bean pot. Keep the beans covered with liquid at all times, but do not cover the pot with a lid. Simmer on stove over low fire all day.

CALIFORNIA SPAGHETTI SAUCE

1 large ONION
1 GARLIC CLOVE
2 lbs. lean GROUND BEEF
½ to 1 lb. ground SAUSAGE
2 cans (303) STEWED TOMATOES
1 can (8 oz.) TOMATO SAUCE
1 can (10½ oz.) BEEF CONSOMME (or homemade stock)
1 cup RED WINE
1 tablespoon SUGAR
OREGANO (pinch or two)
SALT and PEPPER

Combine tomatoes, tomato sauce, consomme, wine, sugar in a large saucepan. Slice and lightly brown garlic and onion in iron skillet. Then add to sauce. In same skillet brown ground meat (breaking up and stirring around). Add salt, pepper and oregano. Add to sauce and simmer several hours (skimming off fat). Sauce may be used over spaghetti, linguini, or as filling for green peppers topped with cheese.

To Broil Tomatoes

Wash tomatoes, but do not peel. Cut crosswise in half and dip surfaces in melted butter, flour, and cornmeal. Set halves in baking pan, cut side up, and broil til tomatoes are browned on top.

GLAZED WESTERN CARROTS

12 small CARROTS (peeled)
2 tablespoons BUTTER
1/3 cup HONEY
1 tablespoon LEMON JUICE
½ cup crushed PINEAPPLE (drained)

Cook whole carrots, covered, in small amount of boiling salted water til just tender. Melt butter in shallow pan; add honey, lemon juice, and pineapple. Add carrots and turn to coat evenly. Bake at 350 F for 8 to 10 minutes, or cook over low heat til well glazed. (Makes 4 servings)

CALIFORNIA SPICE CAKE

1 cup RAW CARROT (grated)
¾ cup RAW POTATO (grated)
2½ cups sifted all-purpose FLOUR
1½ teaspoons BAKING POWDER
½ teaspoon BAKING SODA
½ teaspoon SALT
2½ teaspoons Pumpkin Pie SPICE
¼ teaspoon CLOVES
1½ cups SALAD OIL
2¼ cups SUGAR
4 EGG YOLKS
5 tablespoons hot WATER
1 cup PECANS (chopped)
4 EGG WHITES

Measure flour; sift with baking powder, soda, salt and spices. Dredge grated carrot and potato with a half cup of flour mixture. In a large electric mixing bowl, cream oil and sugar together til well blended. Add egg yolks, one at a time, and beat well after each addition. Add hot water and flour mixture gradually. Add grated raw vegetables and pecans. Beat egg whites til soft peaks form and fold into batter. Fill pans 2/3 full with batter. (Baking time depends on size of pan. Batter will fill three 9-inch layer pans, or a 10-inch heavy tubed cake pan, or variety of vegetable or fruit cans. Allow 30 minutes for layer pans and fruit cans; about an hour for tube pan. Use a pre-heated 350 F oven.) Cool in pan for 10 minutes, remove, and complete cooling on wire rack. Frost and serve.

WESTERN CAULIFLOWER

Wash a head of cauliflower well, leaving whole with some of the green leaves around the base. Cook, covered, in small amount of boiling, salted water until tender (about 20 to 30 minutes). Drain and serve with sauce.

SAUCE

½ small ONION
½ small GREEN PEPPER
1 stalk CELERY
1 tablespoon BUTTER
½ can (10½ oz.) condensed TOMATO SOUP
1 2-oz. can sliced MUSHROOMS
1 tablespoon chopped PIMIENTO
1 tablespoon chopped PARSLEY
1/8 teaspoon SALT

Chop onion and green pepper fine; cut celery into thin slices. Heat butter in saucepan, toss in vegetables and saute til onions are golden brown. Stir in tomato soup, mushrooms and liquid, pimiento and salt. Simmer til heated through. (Makes 1 cup)

CARROT BREAD

3 cups SUGAR
2¼ cups cooking OIL
4½ cups FLOUR
3 teaspoons each:
BAKING POWDER, BAKING SODA, CINNAMON, NUTMEG
3 cups CARROTS (grated)
6 EGGS
3 teaspoons VANILLA
1½ cups PECANS

Mix sugar and oil. Add flour sifted with dry ingredients. Add carrots, then eggs (one at a time), beating well after each addition. Stir in vanilla, then nuts, blending well. Pour into four lightly oiled 9x5x3 loaf pans; bake in 370 F oven for 50 to 60 minutes. (Makes 4 loaves)

CARROT CAKE

1½ cups OIL
2 cups SUGAR
4 EGG YOLKS
2 cups CARROTS (grated)
4 tablespoons hot WATER
½ cup NUTS (chopped)
2¼ cups all-purpose FLOUR
2½ teaspoons CINNAMON
1½ teaspoons NUTMEG
1½ teaspoons BAKING SODA
½ teaspoon SALT
4 EGG WHITES

Combine oil and sugar and mix well. Beat egg yolks separately; add carrots and hot water. Mix well and add to oil and sugar mixture. Sift flour with cinnamon, nutmeg, soda and salt twice and add to carrot mixture. Add nuts. Fold in egg whites and pour into greased and floured 13x9 pan. Bake in 350 F oven 1 1/4 hours (or til cake tests done). Cool and frost in pan.

Cream Cheese Frosting

1 (8-oz.) pkg. CREAM CHEESE
¼ lb. BUTTER (softened)
1 lb. POWDERED SUGAR
1 teaspoon VANILLA

Blend cream cheese and butter til light and fluffy; add sugar and vanilla and cream mixture to spreading consistency. (If necessary, add milk to thin frosting.)

PUMPKIN PIE

2 EGGS (slightly beaten)
1½ cups PUMPKIN
¾ cup SUGAR
½ teaspoon SALT
1 teaspoon CINNAMON
¼ teaspoon NUTMEG
½ teaspoon GINGER
1½ cups EVAPORATED MILK
1 unbaked 9" PIE CRUST

Combine beaten eggs with pumpkin and stir til smooth. Add sugar and mix again. Add salt, cinnamon, nutmeg, ginger, evaporated milk and continue stirring. Pour into 9-inch unbaked pastry shell. Bake for 15 minutes in 425 F oven; reduce oven heat to 350 F and continue baking for another 45 minutes.

WHEAT GERM ZUCCHINI BREAD

1¼ cups vacuum packed WHEAT GERM
3 cups FLOUR
3 teaspoons BAKING POWDER
1 teaspoon SALT
2 teaspoons CINNAMON
1 cup chopped NUTS
2 EGGS
1¾ cups SUGAR
2 teaspoons pure VANILLA EXTRACT
2/3 cup COOKING OIL
3 cups grated ZUCCHINI (about 3 medium)

Mix together wheat germ, flour, baking powder, salt, cinnamon and nuts. Beat eggs til light colored and fluffy. Beat in sugar, vanilla and oil. Stir in zucchini. Gradually stir in wheat germ mixture. Turn into 2 greased, floured 8 1/2 x 4 1/2 x 2 1/2 loaf pans. Bake in 350 F oven one hour (or til pick comes out clean). If using glass pans, bake at 325 F.

PUMPKIN LOAF

3 1/3 cups all purpose FLOUR (sifted)
2 teaspoons BAKING SODA
1½ teaspoons SALT
1 teaspoon CINNAMON
1 teaspoon NUTMEG
4 EGGS
2/3 cup WATER
3 cups SUGAR
2 cups canned PUMPKIN
1 cup COOKING OIL (or melted shortening)

Combine flour, baking soda, salt, cinnamon and nutmeg in mixing bowl and mix well. In a separate bowl, beat eggs well, add sugar, pumpkin and oil and mix completely. Add flour mixture to pumpkin mix. Pour into two loaf pans and bake in 350 F oven for 50-60 minutes. (Chopped nuts may be added immediately after addition of flour, if desired.)

ALMOND BAKED CELERY

1 bunch CELERY (thinly sliced)
½ cup chopped, blanched, lightly toasted ALMONDS
½ cup grated sharp AMERICAN CHEESE
1 teaspoon SALT
1/8 teaspoon PEPPER
½ teaspoon PAPRIKA
2 10½-oz. cans CREAM OF CELERY SOUP
½ cup buttered CRUMBS

Place celery in buttered 9-inch square pan; cover with chopped nuts, then grated cheese. Combine seasonings and soup; pour over all. Top with crumbs. Bake at 375 F for 40-45 minutes.

To Cook Greens

To cook beet and turnip tops, chicory, collards, dandelion, kale, mustard, spinach, and swiss chard: cut off roots, remove any damaged leaves. Wash thoroughly in running cool water. Put leaves in colander. Set colander over a pan of boiling water and cover. Let the steam wilt and tenderize the leaves. Steam for 5 to 25 minutes (depending on type of greens). Season with salt and pepper and serve with vinegar or lemon juice.

CAESAR SALAD

3 qts. SALAD GREENS (bite sized)
1 clove GARLIC
½ cup SALAD OIL
½ cup PARMESAN CHEESE
¼ cup BLUE CHEESE
1 tablespoon WORCESTERSHIRE SAUCE
½ teaspoon DRY MUSTARD
¼ teaspoon SALT
1/8 teaspoon PEPPER
1 EGG
½ cup fresh LEMON JUICE
2 cups crisp garlic flavored CROUTONS

Put crisp, cold salad greens into large, chilled salad bowl that has been rubbed with a clove of garlic. Add oil, cheeses, Worcestershire, mustard, salt and pepper. Break raw egg over greens and pour in lemon juice. Toss thoroughly, so every leaf is coated with seasonings. On the last toss, add croutons and serve. (Makes 8 servings)

POTATO SALAD a la PACIFIC

3 large POTATOES
1/3 cup dry WHITE WINE
3 tablespoons SALAD OIL
1½ teaspoons LEMON JUICE
2 tablespoons minced ONION
½ medium CUCUMBER (diced)
2 tablespoons chopped GREEN PEPPER
¼ cup melted BUTTER
1 teaspoon SALT
PEPPER to taste

Boil potatoes in their jackets until tender. Peel and dice or slice. Combine remaining ingredients; pour over potatoes and toss thoroughly. Chill for several hours before serving, tossing occasionally so all pieces are well marinated. Serve in lettuce cups, garnished with tomato wedges. (Makes 4 servings)

WESTERN ASPIC MOLD

2 head western iceberg LETTUCE
2 envelopes plain GELATIN
¾ teaspoon SALT
1 cup cold WATER (or chicken stock)
1 can (1 pint 2 oz.) TOMATO JUICE
3 tablespoons LEMON JUICE
1 tablespoon grated ONION
Few dashes TABASCO
1 can (4½ or 5 oz.) medium deveined SHRIMP
1/3 cup finely chopped DILL PICKLE

Core, rinse and drain lettuce; chill in plastic bag. Dissolve gelatin and salt in water, stirring over medium heat. Stir in tomato juice, lemon juice, onion, and Tabasco. Chill til mixture begins to thicken. Meanwhile, cut lettuce lengthwise into halves and shred across heart to make one quart. Chill all but 2 cups shredded lettuce in plastic bag. Rinse and drain shrimp. Fold 2 cups shredded lettuce, shrimp and pickle into gelatine mixture; turn into 6-cup mold. Chill til firm. Unmold onto platter, and arrange remaining 2 cups shredded lettuce around edge.

ICEBERG-KABUKI

1 head western iceberg LETTUCE
2 large or 3 small TOMATOES (sliced)
1 cup drained canned BEAN SPROUTS
½ cup CORN OIL
¼ cup VINEGAR
3 tablespoons TOMATO PASTE
1 tablespoon Kikkoman SOY SAUCE
1 teaspoon ACCENT
½ teaspoon SALT
½ teaspoon ground GINGER
¾ cup sliced CELERY
¼ cup coarsley chopped ONION

Core, rinse and drain lettuce; chill in disposable plastic bag. Cut head lengthwise into halves; place cut sides down on board and coarsely shred crosswise to yield 5 cups. Combine with tomatoes and bean sprouts in salad bowl. To make dressing, combine all other ingredients in electric blender; process at medium speed 3 to 5 seconds til celery is finely grated. Spoon some dressing into center of salad; toss at table. (Serves 6)

WINTER LETTUCE SALAD

1 head iceberg LETTUCE
2 cups GARBANZO BEANS (drained)
3 slices BACON (diced)
1 beaten EGG
2 GREEN ONIONS (chopped fine)
1 tablespoon SUGAR
½ teaspoon SALT
¼ cup garlic-flavored VINEGAR
2 tablespoons WATER
¼ teaspoon dried SAVORY

Wash, drain and tear lettuce into bite-size pieces. Drain beans and heat. Fry bacon til crisp. Pour off excess fat except for 2 tablespoons. Combine egg, onion, sugar, salt, vinegar, and savory and add to bacon. Heat to boiling point. Pour over lettuce and toss. Add hot beans and serve immediately.

HONG KONG APPLE SALAD

2 cups peeled, diced Newton Pippin APPLES
2 teaspoons LEMON JUICE
2 cups diced cooked TONGUE (or ham)
1 can or jar (11 oz.) MANDARIN ORANGES (drained)
1 can (1 lb.) WHITE KIDNEY BEANS
SALAD GREENS

Sprinkle apples with lemon juice and toss to mix. Combine with remainder of ingredients and arrange on lettuce leaves. Serve dressing separately.

Piquante Dressing

½ cup MAYONNAISE
1 cup dairy SOUR CREAM
½ teaspoon SUGAR
1½ teaspoons grated ONION
2 teaspoons CURRY POWDER
½ teaspoon SALT

Combine all ingredients and serve with Apple Salad.

GRECIAN-STYLE SALAD

1 head western iceberg LETTUCE
½ cup RADISH SLICES
½ cup chopped GREEN ONION
1/3 cup OIL (part olive, part corn)
2 tablespoons LEMON JUICE
2 teaspoons SUGAR
½ teaspoon SALT
Few dashes PEPPER
4 oz. Feta or Romano CHEESE
1 can (2 oz.) flat ANCHOVY FILETS (drained)
About 2/3 cup whole pitted OLIVES
Crumbled dry OREGANO

Core, rinse and drain lettuce; chill in plastic bag. Cut head lengthwise into halves; place cut sides down on board and shred crosswise. Then chop to yield 5 cups. Combine chopped lettuce with radishes and onion in salad bowl. Mix oil, lemon juice, sugar and salt with pepper to taste. Toss with greens mixture. Crumble cheese coarsely and sprinkle over salad near rim of bowl. Wrap each anchovy around an olive and place inside ring of cheese. Sprinkle oregano over all and toss. (Serves 6)

HOT POTATO SALAD

4 lbs. small white POTATOES
1 cup diced BACON
½ cup minced ONION
1½ tablespoons CORNSTARCH
¼ cup SUGAR
4 teaspoons SALT
¼ teaspoon PEPPER
¾ cup VINEGAR
1½ cups WATER
¼ cup snipped PARSLEY
1 cup diced CELERY

Cook potatoes in jackets in boiling, salted water til fork tender. Peel and slice into 1/4 inch slices. In a skillet, fry bacon til crisp. Add minced onion and saute til just tender, not brown. In a bowl, mix cornstarch, sugar, salt and pepper. Stir in vinegar and water and mix til smooth. Add to bacon and onion, stirring over low heat until slightly thickened. Pour this hot dressing over potatoes, parsley and celery which have been combined into a bowl. Toss and serve hot. (Makes 8 servings)

MONTEREY TUNA SALAD

1 teaspoon SALT
1 teaspoon DRY MUSTARD
1 teaspoon grated ONION
2 tablespoons chopped PARSLEY
6 tablespoons LEMON JUICE
½ cup Salad OIL
¼ cup chopped PIMIENTO
1 can (14 oz.) ARTICHOKE HEARTS (drained)
2 cans (6½ or 7 oz. each) TUNA
¼ lb. Monterey Jack CHEESE (cut in strips)
½ cup pitted ripe OLIVES
8 SCALLIONS

In small bowl mix together salt, dry mustard, onion, parsley, lemon juice, oil and pimiento. Add artichoke hearts, cover and chill several hours. To serve, remove artichokes with slotted spoon and arrange on platter with tuna chunks, cheese, olives and scallions. Serve with reserved marinade. (Serves 4)

MEXICAN SALAD

2 large GREEN PEPPERS (1 inch chunks)
1 medium ONION (in chunks)
4 medium TOMATOES (peeled and cut into chunks)
½ cup CELERY (chopped)
4 sllces BACON (fried crisp and crumbled)
4 hard cooked EGGS (sliced)
½ teaspoon SALT
1 teaspoon CHILI POWDER
½ cup VINEGAR

Toss together green pepper, onion, tomato, celery, bacon, eggs and salt. Heat chili powder and vinegar to boiling and pour over all ingredients. Toss lightly and serve on crisp lettuce. (Makes 6 servings)

WESTERN VEGETABLE SALAD

½ cup OIL
¼ cup LEMON JUICE
2 teaspoons SUGAR
1 teaspoon SALT
½ teaspoon ground CUMIN
1 clove GARLIC (crushed)
6 large TOMATOES
2 CUCUMBERS (peeled and thinly sliced)
2/3 cup ONION (minced)
1 GREEN PEPPER (diced)
1 cup pitted ripe OLIVES

Prepare dressing by blending together oil, lemon juice, sugar, salt and cumin. Spear garlic on wood picks and put into dressing. Let dressing stand at least 2 hours before mixing with salad. Remove garlic. (Makes 3/4 cup). One hour before serving, cut tomatoes in 3/4'' chunks. Mix with remaining salad ingredients in large salad bowl. Add enough dressing so vegetables are moist. Marinate for 1 hour. (Makes 8 servings)

STUFFED TOMATO SALAD

6 medium sized ripe TOMATOES
½ cup chopped CELERY
½ cup chopped CUCUMBER
1 tablespoon minced ONION
1 tablespoon chopped GREEN PEPPER
2 hard cooked EGGS (chopped)
2 tablespoons MAYONNAISE
¼ teaspoon PEPPER
1 teaspoon SALT

Wash the tomatoes and remove stem ends. Scoop out the centers, leaving shells about 1/4-inch thick. Turn upside down on plate to drain. Dice the tomato pulp and combine with other ingredients. Then stuff the tomatoes with the mixture and serve on lettuce leaves or bed of watercress. (Makes 6 servings)

WILTED LETTUCE

6 slices BACON (diced)
1 head LETTUCE
1 tomato (diced)
¼ cup diced GREEN ONION
½ teaspoon SALT
½ teaspoon OREGANO
¼ teaspoon PEPPER
2 tablespoons VINEGAR

Fry bacon til crisp. Drain, reserving tablespoon of fat. Tear lettuce into bowl and add all ingredients except vinegar. Combine vinegar and bacon fat in pan and bring to boil. Toss with salad. Crumble bacon bits over salad.

PONDEROSA COLE SLAW

1 cup mild flavored HONEY
1 cup WINE VINEGAR
½ cup finely chopped ONION
1 teaspoon SALT
1 teaspoon CELERY SEED
1 large head CABBAGE (finely chopped, 4 cups)
1 cup diced GREEN PEPPER
1 cup diced CELERY

In a small saucepan, combine honey with vinegar, onion, salt, and celery seed. Bring to boil, reduce heat and simmer five minutes. Cool. Pour the cooled dressing over prepared vegetables and toss lightly. Cover and chill several hours or overnight to blend flavors.

CELESTIAL CARROT SALAD

½ lb. CARROTS, grated (about 2 cups)
1 tablespoon fresh LEMON JUICE
1/8 teaspoon SALT
¼ cup miniature MARSHMALLOWS
1 can (8½ oz.) PINEAPPLE TIDBITS
1 tablespoon HONEY
¼ teaspoon NUTMEG
½ cup plain YOGURT or dairy SOUR CREAM

Combine grated carrots, lemon juice and salt. Add marshmallows and fruit. Blend honey and nutmeg with yogurt. Toss lightly with carrot mixture. Chill well. (Add 1/4 cup shredded coconut to carrot mixture before adding dressing, if desired.)

WESTERN WHOPPER

1 head western iceberg LETTUCE
2 TANGERINES
3 tablespoons SALAD OIL
2 tablespoons VINEGAR
2 tablespoons CORN SYRUP
½ teaspoon SEASONED SALT
¼ teaspoon CELERY SEED
1/8 teaspoon PEPPER
½ cup ONION RINGS
2 cups torn SPINACH LEAVES

Core, rinse and drain lettuce. Chill in plastic pag. Peel and section tangerines; cut each section crosswise in half and remove seeds. Mix oil, vinegar, syrup and seasonings in small bowl or jar. Add tangerines and onion rings and marinate for 30 minutes. Tear enough lettuce into bite-size pieces to measure one quart; combine with spinach in salad bowl. Pour dressing mixture over and toss. Serve at once. (Makes 6 servings)

SOUR CREAM DRESSING

1 cup SOUR CREAM
2 tablespoons VINEGAR
1 tablespoon fresh LEMON JUICE
1 tablespoon GREEN ONION (minced)
½ teaspoon SALT
3 tablespoons SUGAR

Blend together all ingredients and chill. (Makes 1 1/4 cups)

FRESH FRUIT DRESSING

½ cup SALAD OIL
¼ cup fresh LEMON JUICE
2 tablespoons HONEY
1 teaspoon SALT

Blend together all ingredients and chill. (Makes about 3/4 cup)

California Sea Food

Baked, barbecued, boiled, broiled, fried, grilled, poached, salted, steamed, stewed -- fish, a delicious, nutritious dish. Since fish have little connective tissue, cooking time is almost nil -- when fish flakes at the touch of a fork, it's ready to be served. Fish can be purchased canned, fresh, frozen, kippered, pickled and smoked.

Cooking styles depend on the type of fish selected. Ideal for baking or broiling are albacore, bocaccio, black sea bass and white sea bass, bonito, barracuda, cod, flying fish, halibut, mackerel, rock cod and the varieties of rockfish, sablefish, salmon, shad, sheepshead (also known as California red fish), steelhead, swordfish, whitefish and yellowtail. Frying is recommended for catfish, flounder, pompano, rock bass, trout, black and striped bass, and sole. Broiling is suggested for albacore, flying fish, grunion, halibut, herring, mullets, mackerel, salmon, sculpin, smelts, and tuna.

California halibut is a particularly versatile fish. Actually, a large flounder, this fish may be prepared in a variety of ways, and is ideal for fish loaves, fish salads, and fish stews. Fish may be served with a basic white sauce or melted butter with chopped parsley and lemon slices.

Grunion running is an exciting event. Tiny fish fling themselves in wild abandonment on the southern California beaches at high tide. Natives and visitors alike flock to the water's edge in the evening hours, flashlight in hand, scooping grunion into buckets and pots.

Shellfish include abalone, clams, crabs, lobster, oysters and shrimp. Abalone, a single-shelled mollusk found only on the Pacific Coast, is extracted from its shell, pounded, and sliced for frying. Clams may be dug along the coast with a shovel, dumped into a bucket, later to be steamed and savored. Pacific Coast crabs are majestic in size; about a dozen Atlantic coast crabs would be needed to produce the same amount of meat as a good-sized California crab. Lobsters, on the other hand, are smaller than their Atlantic relatives, and do not boast large claws. They are commonly referred to as spiny lobsters.

Oysters, a popular seafood, are low in calories and high in nutrition, and may be used in any recipes which feature clams, blending well in casseroles and chowders.

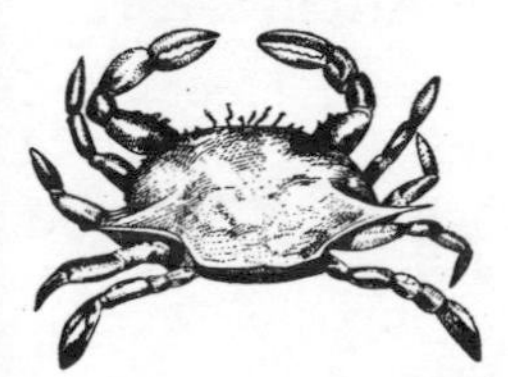

Scallops, which belong to the shellfish family, are commonly sold without their shells. Like the tiny California shrimp, they need minimal cooking time and lend themselves well to cocktails, salads, soups, and omelettes.

Fish

PAN-FRIED FISH

2 lbs. FISH STEAKS or FILLETS
1 teaspoon SALT
1/8 teaspoon PEPPER
1 EGG
1 tablespoon MILK or WATER
1 cup CRUMBS (bread or cracker) or Cornmeal or Flour

(Thaw frozen fish.) Cut fish into serving portions. Sprinkle both sides with salt and pepper. Beat egg slightly and blend in milk. Dip fish in egg; roll in crumbs. Melt fat in heavy frypan. (Fat should be hot, not smoking.) Fry fish til brown on one side; turn fish and brown other side (total cooking time 8 to 10 minutes). Drain; serve plain or with sauce. (Makes 6 servings)

PAN-DRESSED FISH

3 lbs. pan-dressed FISH (fresh or frozen)
¼ cup MILK
1 EGG (beaten)
1 teaspoon SALT
1½ cups dry bread, cereal, or cracker CRUMBS
FAT for frying

(Thaw frozen fish.) Clean, wash, and dry fish. Combine milk, egg, salt and pepper. Dip fish in milk; roll in crumbs. Place fish in single layer in hot fat in 10-inch frypan. Fry at moderate heat five minutes (or til brown). Turn carefully and fry five minutes longer (or til fish flakes). Drain and serve.

OVEN-FRIED FISH

2 lbs. FISH FILLETS (or STEAKS) (fresh or frozen)
½ cup MILK
1 teaspoon SALT
1½ cups dry bread CRUMBS
¼ cup melted FAT

(Thaw frozen fish.) Cut fish into portions. Combine milk and salt. Dip fish in milk; roll in crumbs. Place fish in single layer, skin side down, on well-greased baking pan. Pour fat over fish and bake at 500 F for 10 minutes (or til fish flakes). (Serves 6)

BAKED FISH FILLETS

1 lb. FISH FILLETS (fresh or frozen)
½ can CREAM of MUSHROOM SOUP
½ cup MILK
¼ teaspoon SALT
Dash PEPPER
¼ teaspoon GARLIC SALT

(Thaw frozen fish.) Cut fillets into six serving pieces and place in baking dish. Combine soup, milk, and spices and pour over fish. Dot with butter and bake in 350 F oven for 20 minutes. Serve with sprigs of parsley and lemon wedges.

BROILED FISH STEAKS

2 lbs. FISH FILLETS
(or STEAKS) (fresh or frozen)
2 tablespoons melted FAT
2 tablespoons LEMON JUICE
1 teaspoon SALT
½ teaspoon PAPRIKA

(Thaw frozen fish.) Cut fish into portions. Sprinkle both sides with salt and pepper. Place fish in a single layer, skin side down, on well-greased baking pan. (Preheat broiler and pan 5 to 8 minutes before greasing.) Combine remaining ingredients and mix well. Pour over fish. Broil about 3 inches from heat for 10 minutes (or til fish flakes easily). Baste once or twice during broiling with sauce in pan. (Serves 6)

POACHED FISH

2 lbs FISH FILLETS
or STEAKS (fresh or frozen)
2 cups boiling WATER
¼ cup LEMON JUICE
1 small ONION (thinly sliced)
1 teaspoon SALT
3 PEPPERCORNS
2 sprigs PARSLEY
1 BAY LEAF
EGG SAUCE
PAPRIKA

(Thaw frozen fish.) Remove skin and bones from fish. Cut fish into portions. Place fish in well-greased 10-inch frypan. Add remaining ingredients. Cover and simmer 5 to 10 minutes (or til fish flakes easily). Remove carefully to heated platter. Pour Egg Sauce over fish, sprinkle with paprika, and serve. (Serves 6)

Egg Sauce

¼ cup BUTTER
2 tablespoons FLOUR
¾ teaspoon DRY MUSTARD
½ teaspoon SALT
Dash PEPPER
1¼ cups MILK
2 hard-cooked EGGS (chopped)
1 tablespoon PARSLEY (chopped)

Melt butter, stir in flour and seasonings. Add milk gradually, and cook til thick and smooth. Stir constantly. Add eggs and parsley and heat.

PLANKED FISHSTEAKS

3 lbs. FISH (dressed)
1½ teaspoons SALT
1/8 teaspoon PEPPER
4 tablespoons BUTTER
Mashed POTATOES
Cooked Vegetables:
PEAS, CARROTS, CAULIFLOWER,
TOMATOES, or ONIONS

(Use hardwood plank; oil well, and place in cold oven. Heat plank thoroughly during preheating period.) Thaw frozen fish; clean, wash and dry fresh fish. Sprinkle inside and out with salt and pepper. Brush with melted fat. Set fish on hot oiled plank (or greased metal platter). Bake in 350 F oven 45 minutes (or til fish flakes easily). Remove from oven; arrange border of mashed potatoes around fish. Place in preheated broiler til potatoes are slightly browned. Remove from oven; arrange other hot vegetables around fish. Garnish with parsley and lemon.

STEAMED FISH

1½ lbs. FISH FILLETS or STEAKS (fresh or frozen)
1 qt. boiling WATER
1½ teaspoons SALT

(Thaw frozen fish.) Place fish in well-greased steamer insert pan. Sprinkle fish with salt. Bring water to boiling point, insert steamer pan and cover tightly. (Spices or wine may be added to water at this point before covering.) Steam for 5 to 10 minutes. Cool, remove skin and bones. Steamed fish may be served with sauce or chilled and flaked for salads. (Makes 2 cups)

BAKED, STUFFED FISH

1 dressed FISH (3 lbs. fresh or frozen)
SALT and PEPPER
STUFFING
2 tablespoons melted FAT

(Thaw frozen fish.) Clean, wash, and dry fresh fish. Sprinkle inside and out with salt. Stuff fish loosely and close with skewers. Place fish in greased bakingpan and brush with melted fat. Bake at 350 F for 45 to 60 minutes (or til fish flakes).

Fish Stuffing

½ cup CELERY (chopped)
¼ cup ONION (chopped)
¼ cup BUTTER (melted)
1 qt. dry BREAD CUBES
1 EGG (beaten)
½ teaspoon SALT
¼ teaspoon THYME

Heat butter and saute all ingredients; stuff fish and bake.

FISH LOAF

2½ cups flaked, cooked FISH
3 EGGS
½ cup soft BREAD CRUMBS
1 tablespoon melted SHORTENING
1 teaspoon SALT
1/8 teaspoon PEPPER
1 tablespoon PARSLEY (minced)

Separate the eggs, beat the yolks til lemon-colored and the whites til stiff. Flake the fish and add it with the remaining ingredients to the egg yolks. Fold in the egg whites and bake in greased loaf pan at 350 F for 40-45 minutes.

CALIFORNIA CIOPPINO

1 ONION (chopped)
2 cloves GARLIC (chopped)
2 tablespoons PARSLEY (chopped)
Cooking OIL
4 fresh TOMATOES (chopped)
¼ cup TOMATO JUICE
2 lbs. ROCKFISH (cut in bite-size pieces)

Lightly brown onion, garlic and parsley in frypan (about five minutes). Add tomato juice and tomatoes and simmer about 15 minutes. Add fish and simmer about 20 minutes (stirring occasionally). Serve steaming hot in soup bowls.

CEVICHE (Seviche)

2 lbs. FRESH FISH (skinned)
(Bass, Rock Cod)
2 cups LIME JUICE
1 ONION (chopped)
2 TOMATOES (chopped)
3 tablespoons OLIVE OIL
2 teaspoons WHITE VINEGAR
½ teaspoon OREGANO
½ cup JALAPENO PEPPERS
(or GREEN PEPPERS) (diced)
2 tablespoons PARSLEY (chopped)

Cut fish into cubes and marinate in lime juice. Cover bowl and store in refrigerator for 4 to 6 hours. (Lime juice cooks the fish.) Drain lime juice and dry fish cubes. Combine other ingredients and pour over cubes. Chill thoroughly.

SEASIDE GRUNION

2 to 3 lbs. GRUNION (pan-ready)
2 teaspoons SALT
Chopped ONION and PARSLEY
3 strips BACON

Clean, wash, and dry fish. Cut 6 squares of heavy-duty aluminum foil (each 12 x 12). Grease lightly. Divide fish on foil, sprinkle with salt and pepper; add onion and parsley. Top with bacon strips (cut in half). Seal packages and close edges with double folds. Set packages on grill about 4 inches from hot coals. Cook about 10 minutes, open packages, serve. (This recipe can be used for smelt and other tiny fish.)

PICKLED HERRING (Marinated Herring)

1 cup VINEGAR
1 tablespoon
PICKLING SPICES
3 tablespoons SUGAR
1 ONION (sliced)
HERRINGS (2 or 3)

Remove heads and scales from herrings. Wash well and soak in bowl of cold water overnight in refrigerator. Drain, slit down bellies, remove entrails but save the milch (fish sperm). Herrings may be skinned and filleted (starting at the tail) by removing meat from backbone. Cut herring meat into two-inch slices. Using a 2-quart glass jar or crock, alternate herring slices with onion slices. (Unpeeled lemon slices may also be alternated.) Topmost layer should be onion slices. Mash the milch and strain into vinegar marinade. Pour over herring, cover jar, and store in refrigerator from 5 to 7 days. (Serves 6. Herring slices may be served with sour cream, if desired.)

BASIC WHITE SAUCE

1 tablespoon BUTTER
1 tablespoon FLOUR
¼ teaspoon SALT
1 cup MILK

Melt butter. Add flour and salt, mixing to smooth paste. Simmer (about one minute). Remove from heat; slowly add 1/2 the milk. Stir til blended. Return to heat; stir til mixture thickens. Add remaining milk; heat til mixture is smooth and creamy. (For a thicker sauce, double butter and flour measurements.)

SEA WORLD CIOPPINO

Atlantis Restaurant -- courtesy of Chef Nick Recio

- 6 fresh TOMATOES (Chopped)
- 1 SHALLOT (chopped)
- 1 clove GARLIC (minced)
- ½ BAY LEAF
- 1 pinch OREGANO
- 4 oz. BURGUNDY WINE
- 1 Dungeness CRAB (broken in half, legs separated, claws cracked)
- 6 large SHRIMP (in shell)
- 6 oz. fresh ocean FISH (swordfish, sea bass, cut in 1½ inch squares)

Combine tomatoes, shallot, garlic, bay leaf, oregano and red wine in saucepan; simmer about 30 minutes (or til liquid is reduced by half). Place all the uncooked sea food in a covered pan and add sauce. Cover, bring to a boil; reduce heat and simmer 15 minutes. (Serves 2)

BOILED SHRIMP

Boiling is the basic method of cooking raw shrimp; 1 1/2 pounds of raw shrimp yields about 3/4 pound of cooked shrimp.

Boiling Before Peeling

- 1½ lbs. SHRIMP
- 1 qt. of WATER
- ¼ cup SALT

Wash shrimp. Place in boiling salted water, cover and return to boiling point. Simmer five minutes. Drain, peel, remove veins, wash, and chill.

Boiling After Peeling

- 1½ lbs. SHRIMP
- 1 qt. WATER
- 2 tablespoons SALT

To peel shrimp, make a shallow cut lengthwise down the back of each shrimp. Wash and place in boiling salted water. Cover and return to boiling point. Simmer five minutes; drain and remove any particles of sand veins remaining. Chill.

SHELLFISH NEWBURG

- 3 tablespons BUTTER
- 2 cups fresh or canned SHELLFISH (lobster, crab or shrimp)
- SALT and PAPRIKA
- ½ cup Calif. SHERRY
- 2 EGG YOLKS
- ½ cup CREAM

Melt butter in saucepan. Add shellfish, season with salt and paprika, and saute gently for 5 minutes. Add wine and simmer 5 minutes. Beat egg yolks and cream together; add to shellfish mixture and cook, stirring gently, just til thickened. DO NOT LET MIXTURE BOIL. Serve on hot toast or in patty shells.

HANGTOWN FRY

- 16 medium OYSTERS
- FLOUR
- 8 EGGS (beaten)
- BREAD CRUMBS
- BUTTER (for frying)
- ½ cup MILK

Drain and dry oysters; season, roll in flour, dip in eggs, roll in crumbs. Heat butter in frypan and brown oysters on one side. Add milk, salt and pepper to remaining eggs, beat well and pour over oysters. Cook about a minute, then turn, and cook as for omelet (lifting cooked portion to allow uncooked part to run onto frypan.) Fold and serve with bacon.

OYSTER CASSEROLE

- ¼ lb. BUTTER (melted)
- ½ lb. MUSHROOMS (sliced)
- 2 ONIONS (chopped)
- 2 cups BREAD CRUMBS
- 1 qt. OYSTERS (with juice)
- ½ pt. MILK (or cream)

Melt butter in frypan; saute onions and mushrooms til golden. Layer oysters, onions and mushrooms in greased baking dish, covering each layer with milk. Top with bread crumbs, dot with butter and bake uncovered in 300 F oven 50-60 minutes.

CRACKED CRAB

Toss live, hard-shelled crabs (head first) into boiling salted water and bring to a boil again. Cook gently another 20 minutes, drain and rinse. To serve hot, crack shells by tapping with hammer; break off claws and crack with nutcracker to remove meat. Serve on platter with melted butter or mayonnaise.

STEAMED CLAMS

Scrub live clams (shells should be firmly closed) thoroughly to remove sand (changing water several times). Set scrubbed clams in large pot and add water (about 1/2 cup water to four quarts of clams). Cover tightly, set over low heat, and steam til shells open (about 15 minutes). Pour clam broth into soup bowls; serve clams in shell with side dishes of melted butter.

CLAM FRITTERS

- 1 (7 oz.) can CLAMS (minced)
- 1 EGG
- 1 cup all purpose FLOUR
- ¾ cup CLAM JUICE (or milk)
- ½ teaspoon BAKING POWDER
- ½ tablespoon PARSLEY (minced)
- ¼ teaspoon SALT
- 1/8 teaspoon PEPPER

Sift flour, baking powder, salt and pepper together. Add clam juice or milk and well-beaten egg. Mix well and stir in clams and parsley. Drop by tablespoonfuls into deep boiling fat. Fry til golden brown on all sides and drain fritters before serving.

FRIED ABALONE

Place abalone on chopping block and pound with a mallet to tenderize. (Or, abalone may be sliced and slices pounded separately.) Dip into beaten egg, then in very fine bread crumbs. Heat butter (or olive oil) and panfry abalone steaks quickly (no longer than 1 minute for each side). Turn slices only once and do not overcook. Serve immediately.

GEORGE'S TOMATO-CLAM SAUCE

1 GARLIC CLOVE
1 medium ONION (chopped)
¼ cup COOKING OIL (or butter)
1 No. 303 can TOMATO WEDGES (drained, save juice)
½ GREEN PEPPER (chopped)
1 (6½ oz.) can chopped CLAMS
1 or 2 tablespoons BRANDY
½ teaspoon SUGAR
SALT and PEPPER

Lightly saute garlic clove and onion in oil; add other ingredients (except clams) and simmer for 30 minutes. (Add juice from tomatoes during cooking and stir.) Add chopped clams after 30-minute cooking period; simmer uncovered another 5 to 10 minutes and serve over spaghetti or linguini. (Serves 3) (To serve six, double clams and tomatoes.)

FRIED OYSTERS

1 pint OYSTERS
1 cup dry BREAD CRUMBS
1 teaspoon SALT
½ teaspoon GARLIC SALT
1 EGG
2 tablespoons WATER

Combine crumbs and seasonings. Wash oysters, drain, and dry thoroughly. Dip oysters in crumbs, then into egg (diluted with water) and again into crumbs. Fry lightly for a few minutes in hot shortenining and serve with Tartar Sauce.

Tartar Sauce

1 cup MAYONNAISE
½ teaspoon ONION JUICE
LEMON JUICE

Combine all ingredients, thinning to desired consistency with lemon juice. For variety, add chopped pickle, celery, or capers.

LOBSTER

LOBSTER (about 2 lbs.)
2 qts. boiling WATER (to cover)
2 tablespoons SALT

Bring water and salt to rolling boil. Put live lobsters head first into boiling water. Cover and keep at slow boil 20 to 25 minutes. Drain and plunge into cold water to stop cooking process. Pull off claws, separate tail from body and extract tail meat (removing intestinal canal running along center of tail). Set lobster on back and split body lengthwise with sharp knife (taking care not to break stomach, a hard sack located back of head). Discard stomach. Pick out meat from body with fork; save any lobster roe (coral), and serve chilled with meat.

SAVORY TUNA LOAF

- 2 EGGS
- ½ cup MILK
- 2 cups soft BREAD CRUMBS
- ¼ cup frozen minced ONION
- 1 tablespoon dehydrated PARSLEY FLAKES
- ¼ teaspoon THYME
- 1 teaspoon SALT
- ¼ teaspoon PEPPER
- 3 cans (6½ or 7 oz. each) TUNA

Combine eggs, milk, bread crumbs and seasonings in mixing bowl. Blend together. Add tuna and mix thoroughly. Turn into foil-lined loaf pan. Bake in 375 F oven one hour. Turn loaf onto platter; remove foil. (Turn right side up onto another platter.) Garnish with lemon slices and serve with Parsley Sauce.

Parsley Sauce

- 1 can condensed CREAM OF CELERY SOUP
- ½ cup MILK
- 2 tablespoons chopped PARSLEY

Combine undiluted soup and milk. Stir over low heat til hot. Add parsley.

TUNA PILAF

- 2 cans (6½ or 7 oz. each) TUNA
- 2 SCALLIONS (¼-inch pieces)
- 2 stalks CELERY (¼-inch slices)
- 1 medium GREEN PEPPER (2-inch strips)
- 1 can (3 or 4 oz.) sliced MUSHROOMS (drained)
- 3 cups cooked RICE
- ¼ cup sliced PIMIENTOS
- 1 teaspoon SALT
- ¼ teaspoon each PEPPER and THYME
- 2 teaspoons WORCESTERSHIRE SAUCE

Drain oil from tuna into skillet; heat. Cook scallions, celery and green pepper in hot oil until crisp-tender. Add mushrooms, tuna, rice, pimientos, salt, pepper, thyme and sauce. Toss with fork and heat to serving temperature. (Makes 4 servings)

COLD TUNA GAZPACHO BLANCO

- 3 cups fresh BREAD CRUMBS
- 3½ cups WATER
- 2 cans (6½ or 7 oz. each) TUNA
- 1 large clove GARLIC
- ½ cup blanched ALMONDS
- 1½ teaspoons SALT
- ¼ teaspoon PEPPER
- 3 tablespoons VINEGAR

Combine all ingredients in electric blender container, cover and blend until pureed. Chill. Serve with chopped fresh tomatoes, chopped cucumber and chopped onion. (Makes 5 cups)

TUNA SALAD FILLED TOMATOES

½ cup MAYONNAISE
1 teaspoon Prepared MUSTARD
1 tablespoon LEMON JUICE
2 cans (6½ or 7 oz. each) TUNA
1 cup diced CELERY
4 TOMATOES
¼ cup toasted, slivered ALMONDS

Blend mayonnaise, mustard and lemon juice. Add tuna and celery and toss lightly. Cut tomatoes in sixths 'petal fashion' and fill centers with tuna salad. Serve on salad greens, garnish with toasted almonds.

TUNA SANDWICH SPREAD

1 can (9¼ oz.) TUNA
1/3 cup MAYONNAISE
1 teaspoon minced ONION
¼ teaspoon SALT
1 teaspoon LEMON JUICE
1 teaspoon WORCESTERSHIRE SAUCE
1 tablespoon CAPERS (optional)
¼ cup finely diced CELERY

Drain oil from tuna into mayonnaise and blend well. Add remaining ingredients with tuna. Stir with fork til mixture is of fine consistency. Serve as spread with rye (or other) breads.

TUNA MOUSSE

2 envelopes unflavored GELATINE
1½ cups cold WATER
¼ cup LEMON JUICE
1½ cups MAYONNAISE
2 cups finely diced CELERY
2/3 cup pimiento-stuffed OLIVES
2 cans (6½ or 7 oz. each) TUNA

Sprinkle gelatine on cold water in saucepan to soften. Place over low heat, stirring constantly, til gelatine is dissolved. Remove from heat; stir in lemon juice, and cool. Gradually stir into mayonnaise, blending well. Mix in remaining ingredients. Turn into 6-cup mold or 8 individual molds. Chill till firm. Unmold on salad greens. Serve with favorite dressing.

TUNA STROGANOFF

1 8-oz. pkg. medium NOODLES
2 (6½ oz.) cans chunk TUNA
1 cup YOGURT (plain)
1 cup COTTAGE CHEESE
1 tablespoon WORCESTERSHIRE
1 tablespoon minced ONION
2 teaspoons SALT
1/8 teaspoon PEPPER
1 can (2¼ oz.) Lindsay Sliced OLIVES
½ lb. BACON

Bring two quarts water to a boil. Add one teaspoon salt and package of noodles. Boil 8 minutes and drain. Line bottom of casserole with noodles. Add tuna, cottage cheese, yogurt, Worcestershire, onions, salt, pepper and mix gently. Sprinkle olives on top. Fry 1/2 pound bacon in strips. Cut with sharp knife and sprinkle over casserole mixture. Cover with foil and bake at 350 F for 30-40 minutes. (Makes 6 servings)

California Wine

WINES	CHARACTERISTICS
Appetizer Wines EXAMPLES: **Sherry Vermouth**	Sherry -- nutty flavor, dry to semi-sweet. Vermouth -- aromatic, herb-flavored, is either dry or sweet. Best served chilled ... good with appetizers and soups.
Red Table Wines EXAMPLES: **Claret Burgundy**	Dry (not sweet), slightly tart, to blend with hearty foods. Light to ruby-red in color. Other types: Zinfandel, Cabernet, Pinoit Noir. Excellent with spaghetti, steaks, roasts.
White Table Wines EXAMPLES: **Sauterne Rhine Wine**	Delicate flavors, very dry to semi-sweet, pale straw to deep gold. Serve well-chilled. Other types: Chablis, Riesling, Semillon. Goes especially well with fish, chicken, light main course dishes.
Dessert Wines EXAMPLES: **Port Muscatel**	Sweeter, heavier-bodied than table wines, Port is red, Muscatel is amber in color. Other varieties include Tokay, Angelica and White Port. Good with fruits, nuts, and desserts.
Sparkling Wines EXAMPLES: **Champagne Sparkling Burgundy**	Effervescent. Champagne is pale gold or pink. Sparkling Burgundy is red. Others are Sparkling Moselle, Sauterne. Serve well-chilled. Festive wines--with appetizers, main course, or sweets.

COURTESY: WINE INSTITUTE

Wine Appetizers

SESAME CHEESE LOG

1 (3 oz.) CREAM CHEESE
¼ cup Calif. CHABLIS
¼ teaspoon NUTMEG
¼ teaspoon SALT
¾ lb. JACK CHEESE, grated
1/3 cup toasted SESAME SEEDS

Beat cream cheese until soft. Blend in wine, nutmeg, salt and grated cheese. Shape into log about 10 inches long and 2 inches in diameter. Toast sesame seeds in shallow pan in hot oven (400 F) until golden (about 5 minutes). Sprinkle seeds on waxed paper. Roll cheese logs in seeds, pressing them in gently. Chill until firm, about two hours. (Makes one 1-lb. log).

SHRIMP COCKTAIL

1 cup bottled COCKTAIL SAUCE
1/3 cup Calif. BURGUNDY
¼ cup CREAM
1 teaspoon LEMON JUICE
SALT to taste
2 cups cooked or canned small SHRIMP

Mix sauce, wine, cream, lemon juice, salt. Add shrimp and chill well. Serve in cocktail glasses. Or, put sauce in glasses and hang six large shrimp around edge of each glass.

FRUIT COCKTAIL

½ cup Calif. PORT
¼ cup GRAPE or CURRANT JELLY
1 tablespoon LEMON JUICE
SALT
1 cup pitted canned Royal Anne CHERRIES
1 cup diced canned PINEAPPLE
1 cup diced ORANGE SECTIONS

Heat wine to simmering; add jelly and stir til melted. Remove from heat; add lemon juice and salt. Cool. Combine cherries, pineapple and orange sections (thoroughly drained) in a bowl. Pour wine mixture over fruit. Cover and chill several hours. To serve: heap fruit in cocktail glasses and pour some of the wine mixture over each serving.

ANCHOVY WINE SPREAD

1 can ANCHOVIES, drained
2 (8-oz.) pkgs. CREAM CHEESE
¼ cup Calif. SHERRY
2 tablespoons chopped stuffed GREEN OLIVES

Mash drained anchovies. Soften cheese and blend into fish. Beat in sherry until mixture is smooth. Add olives. Cover and chill several hours to blend flavors. To serve: pile into bowl and place bowl in cracked ice. Garnish with strips of anchovy.

Meats with Wine

OVEN-BARBECUED RIBS

2 lbs. BEEF SHORT RIBS
½ cup Calif. BURGUNDY
1 (8 oz.) can TOMATO SAUCE
2 tablespoons chopped ONION
1½ teaspoons SALT
2 tablespoons WINE VINEGAR
1 tablespoon PREPARED MUSTARD

Trim fat from ribs and rub hot skillet with it. Brown ribs slowly on all sides and drain off fat. Combine all other ingredients and pour over ribs. Cover tightly and bake in a slow oven (300 F) from 1 1/2 to 2 hours, til meat is tender.

ORANGE-HAM SLICE

1 center cut slice HAM (1 to 1½ inches thick)
¼ cup chopped raw ONION
2 medium size ORANGES
¼ cup BROWN SUGAR (packed)
1 medium size LEMON
½ cup Calif. SAUTERNE

Score ham fat edge to prevent curling. Place ham slice in baking dish and sprinkle onion over it. Peel and cut oranges into medium-thick slices. Arrange on ham and sprinkle with brown sugar. Top with thin lemon slices. Pour wine over all. Bake at 375 F til ham is tender, 3/4 to 1 hour.

FLANK STEAK ROSE

1 (1½ lbs.) FLANK STEAK
¾ cup Calif. ROSE
1 large clove GARLIC, crushed
1 teaspoon SALT
1 teaspoon PEPPER

Place meat in medium-size bowl. Combine other ingredients and pour over meat. Cover and marinate in refrigerator from one to two hours. Turn meat several times. Drain, reserving marinade. Brush meat with oil and broil or barbecue quickly. Cut diagonally across grain of meat into thin slices. (Marinade which remains may be used as sauce for flank steak.)

WINE-BRAISED CHOPS

6 thick PORK CHOPS
2 teaspoons Prepared MUSTARD
SALT and PEPPER
Dried DILL or SAGE
BROWN SUGAR
6 thin slices LEMON
1 cup Calif. SAUTERNE

Trim fat from chops and grease skillet with trimmings. Brown chops slowly on both sides; drain off excess fat. Spread with mustard and sprinkle with seasonings and brown sugar. Top chops with lemon slices. Pour sauterne over meat. Cover and cook slowly until tender (about an hour). Remove to hot plate. Skim fat from drippings and thicken drippings slightly with cornstarch mixed with cold water. Spoon sauce over meat.

OLD WEST BEEF STEW

¼ lb. SALT PORK (cubed)
2½ lb. BEEF STEW MEAT (cubed)
2 tablespoons FLOUR
1 cup Calif. BURGUNDY
½ cup WATER
Dash of THYME
SALT and PEPPER
12 small white ONIONS (peeled)
1 bunch CARROTS (cut in sticks)
½ lb. fresh MUSHROOMS (sliced)
2 tablespoons chopped PARSLEY

Cook salt pork slowly until crisp and brown. Add meat and brown on all sides. Sprinkle flour over meat and stir well. Add wine and water, stirring constantly until gravy is thickened and smooth. Add seasonings. Cover and simmer gently for three hours, stirring occasionally. Add vegetables and cook for 45 minutes, til vegetables and meat are tender.

CHILI MIO

1½ lbs. lean GROUND BEEF
1 large ONION, chopped
1 clove GARLIC, chopped
2 tablespoons BACON DRIPPINGS
½ cup WATER
¾ cup Calif. BURGUNDY
1 BEEF BOUILLON CUBE
1 tablespoon CUMIN SEED
1 tablespoon CHILI POWDER
2 teaspoons OREGANO
2 (No. 303) cans RED KIDNEY BEANS

Saute beef, onion and garlic in drippings (or other fat) until meat is no longer red. Stir with fork to break meat into small bits. Add water, wine, bouillon cube and seasonings. Bring to boil, then simmer for 45 minutes (stirring often) until mixture is moist but no longer juicy. Add undrained beans; cover and simmer 5 minutes more. (Makes 4-5 servings)

SWISS STEAK SUPREME

2 lb. thick piece ROUND STEAK
GARLIC, SALT and PAPRIKA
3 tablespoons FLOUR
½ cup Calif. BURGUNDY
1 can (10½ oz.) condensed ONION SOUP

Cut steak into 6 serving pieces. Sprinkle with garlic salt and paprika and thoroughly rub in flour. Brown slowly on both sides in heated shortening. Drain excess fat from pan. Sprinkle in any remaining flour. Add wine and soup. Cover and simmer til tender, about 1 1/2 hours. (Makes 6 servings)

WINEBARBECUE BASTE

½ cup Calif. BURGUNDY
½ cup CHILI SAUCE
¼ cup WATER or BROTH
1 tablespoon grated ONION
1 tablespoon WORCESTERSHIRE
Dash powdered GARLIC

Combine ingredients and simmer together for 5 minutes. Use this sauce to baste meat on barbecue grill or broiler.

BURGUNDY BURGERS

1 lb. GROUND LEAN BEEF
¼ cup Calif. BURGUNDY
1 teaspoon SEASONED SALT
Freshly ground PEPPER
BURGUNDY SAUCE

Combine beef, wine, salt and pepper and mix lightly with fork. Shape into 3 or 4 patties. Broil until done as desired. Remove to hot plates and spoon Burgundy Sauce over each burger.

Burgundy Sauce

2 tablespoons each: BUTTER, SOY SAUCE, chopped green ONIONS
3 tablespoons Calif. BURGUNDY

Heat all ingredients together. Mixture may be thickened by adding a little cornstarch mixed with cold water.

EASY BEEF CASSEROLE

1 lb. STEWING BEEF (2 inch chunks)
½ cup Calif. BURGUNDY
1 (10½ oz.) can undiluted condensed CONSOMME
¾ teaspoon SALT
1/8 teaspoon PEPPER

1 medium size ONION, sliced
¼ cup fine dry BREAD CRUMBS
¼ cup sifted all purpose FLOUR

Combine beef, wine, consomme, salt, pepper, and onion in casserole. Mix flour with crumbs and stir into casserole mixture. Cover and bake in slow oven (300 F) about 3 hours (or til beef is tender) (Makes 4 servings)

CHERRY GLAZED HAM

1 boneless cooked HAM (8-10 lb.)
1 can (1 lb. 4 oz.) CHERRY PIE FILLING
1/3 cup Calif. ROSE
2 tablespoons RED WINE VINEGAR
½ teaspoon DRY MUSTARD
Dash CLOVES

Place ham in shallow baking pan. Bake at 325 F about 2 1/2 to 3 hours (or follow directions on ham wrapper). Combine remaining ingredients and heat together slowly until blended. Pour off drippings from ham, skim off fat and discard. Stir browned ham juices into sauce. Spoon sauce over ham the last 20 minutes of baking.

SEASONING WITH WINE

Any meat recipe which requires liquid in the cooking process may be converted to a wine-flavored recipe by simple substitution. For example: replace 1/4 cup of water for each pound of meat with an equal amount of California red or white table wine. Use red wine for beef, lamb, or game; white for veal or pork.

Poultry with Wine

EASY BAKED CHICKEN

- 2 broiling CHICKENS, split in halves
- ½ cup BUTTER
- ½ cup Calif. SAUTERNE
- 1 teaspoon SALT
- ¼ teaspoon PEPPER
- ½ teaspoon dried TARRAGON
- 2 teaspoons CORNSTARCH

Put chickens in shallow baking pan, skin side up. Melt butter. Add wine, salt, pepper, tarragon. Spoon a little over chicken and bake at 325 F about 1 1/4 hours, basting often with sauce. When chicken is tender and brown, pour off sauce and heat to boiling. Stir in cornstarch mixed with a little cold water. Boil one or two minutes, stirring constantly and spoon over chicken.

BARBECUED CHICKEN

- ½ cup Calif. SHERRY
- 1/3 cup HONEY
- 2 teaspoons CINNAMON
- 2 tablespoons LEMON JUICE
- ½ teaspoon CURRY POWDER
- 1 teaspoon GARLIC SALT

Combine all ingredients and marinate chicken pieces for several hours. Turn pieces occasionally then broil or barbecue until tender, basting with remaining marinade. Watch carefully, for the chicken will brown quickly.

GLAZED CHICKEN

- 1 frying CHICKEN, quartered
- 1 teaspoon SALT
- 1/8 teaspoon PEPPER
- ½ cup ORANGE JUICE
- ½ cup Calif. SHERRY
- ½ teaspoon BASIL
- 1/8 teaspoon NUTMEG

Place seasoned chicken in shallow baking pan, skin side up. Combine remaining ingredients and pour over chicken. Bake at 350 F one hour, basting frequently, til chicken is tender.

HERBED CHICKEN ROSE

- 4 large pieces frying CHICKEN
- ¼ teaspoon GARLIC SALT
- ¼ teaspoon PAPRIKA
- 1 tablespoon FLOUR
- 2 or 3 tablespoons SHORTENING (half butter)
- ¼ teaspoon dried ROSEMARY
- ¼ teaspoon dried BASIL
- ½ cup Calif. ROSE
- ½ cup SOUR CREAM

Dredge chicken with garlic salt, paprika and flour, mixed. Brown on both sides in hot shortening. Sprinkle with herbs; add wine; cover and cook slowly til tender (about 25 minutes). Skim any excess fat from pan liquid. Thicken liquid with 1 1/2 teaspoons cornstarch mixed with one tablespoon water (if desired). Stir in sour cream and serve at once.

GLAZED DUCK with Plum Sauce

1 DUCK (about 5 lbs.)
1 teaspoon SALT
¼ teaspoon PEPPER
1 ONION
1 stalk CELERY
¾ cup Calif. PORT
1 Jar (1 lb. 1 oz.) purple PLUMS
½ BAY LEAF
6 whole CLOVES
2 tablespoons WINE VINEGAR
4 teaspoons CORNSTARCH

Remove giblets from duck. Rub body cavity with salt and pepper. Cut one slice onion for sauce. Place remaining onion and celery inside duck, and pour in 1/4 cup Port. Tie legs close together and tuck wings under body. Place on rack in shallow roasting pan. Roast at 325 F for three hours. Pour off fat from time to time as it accumulates in pan. After duck has roasted three hours, brush with half the reserved glaze. Continue roasting 20 minutes longer, brushing twice with remaining glaze. Reheat sauce with plums and serve.

Plum Sauce

Drain syrup from plums, measure and add water, if necessary, to make a cup. Add to remaining 1/2 cup Port with onion slice, bay leaf, cloves, vinegar, and simmer five minutes. Blend cornstarch with a tablespoon cold water. Stir into sauce. Cook, stirring until sauce clears and thickens. Strain and stir in a dash salt. Set aside 1/2 cup to glaze duck. Reheat sauce with plums and serve in separate dish alongside roasted duck.

TURKEY CREAM STEW

1/3 cup BUTTER
1/3 cup FLOUR
1 cup cream or evaporated MILK
1¼ cups TURKEY or CHICKEN BROTH
2 cups diced cooked TURKEY
¼ cup California SHERRY
1 cup each: drained PEAS, tiny whole WHITE ONIONS, diced CARROTS

Melt butter, stir in flour. Add cream and broth. Cook, stirring constantly, until mixture boils and thickens. Add all other ingredients. Heat gently, but thoroughly. Serve on hot biscuits or with noodles or rice. (Two 10-oz. pkgs. of mixed frozen vegetables, cooked and drained, may be substituted.)

GOLD COAST CHICKEN LIVERS

6 slices BACON
1 lb. CHICKEN LIVERS
½ teaspoon SALT
1/8 teaspoon PEPPER
½ cup sifted all purpose FLOUR
½ cup California SAUTERNE

Fry bacon crisp and drain on paper towels. Measure drippings, returning 1/4 cup to skillet. Dredge chicken livers in mixture of salt, pepper, flour. Brown lightly in bacon fat. Turn heat low, add wine, and cover. Steam for 5 minutes, or til livers are cooked. Crumble bacon and sprinkle with parsley over livers. Serve on hot rice or hot noodles.

Seafoods with Wine

CRAB CHEESE PIE

1 can CRABMEAT
1 unbaked 9-inch PASTRY SHELL
1 cup shredded SWISS CHEESE
3 EGGS
1½ cups MILK
¾ teaspoon SALT
1/3 cup Calif. SAUTERNE
PEPPER to taste
PAPRIKA

Drain crab, and arrange in bottom of pastry shell. Sprinkle cheese over crab. Beat eggs lightly. Stir in milk, salt, wine, and pepper. Pour over cheese in pie shell. Sprinkle with paprika. Bake below center of hot oven (425 F) ten minutes. Turn heat to 350 F and bake 25 minutes longer or til custard is set in center. Cool 10 minutes before cutting. Serve warm. Other fish--shrimp, lobster, cooked halibut or sole--may be used in place of crab. (Makes 6 servings)

FILET OF SOLE FLORENTINE

¼ cup BUTTER
¼ cup FLOUR
1 cup MILK
¼ cup CREAM or EVAPORATED MILK
½ cup California CHABLIS
1 can (4 oz.) MUSHROOMS
¼ cup grated PARMESAN CHEESE
½ teaspoon WORCESTERSHIRE SAUCE
SALT and PEPPER
3 cups chopped, cooked SPINACH
1½ lb. FILET OF SOLE

Melt butter and stir in flour. Add milk, cream, wine and liquid from mushrooms. Cook, stirring constantly, until mixture is thick. Add mushrooms, cheese, Worcestershire sauce, salt and pepper. Spread spinach evenly over the bottom of a greased shallow baking dish (8x12x2). Lay fillets on top of spinach and cover with wine-cream sauce. Bake (375 F) for 25 minutes, or until fish flakes when tested with fork. (Makes 4 servings)

SCAMPI

2 (5-oz.) cans SHRIMP, drained
4 tablespoons BUTTER
1/8 teaspoon GARLIC CHIPS
2 tablespoons PARSLEY FLAKES
½ cup Calif. CHABLIS

Melt butter in skillet. Add garlic, parsley and wine. Heat to simmering, add shrimp and cook over low heat until heated thoroughly (about 5 minutes). Serve with rice as main course.

VERMOUTH MARINADE

California Dry Vermouth makes an excellent marinade for fillets or slices of fish. Use about 3/4 cup of Vermouth for four servings of fish. Marinate about an hour, turning occasionally. Then dry, season fish, and broil. Or, add marinade, cover and simmer gently about five minutes til fish is done.

SCALLOPED OYSTERS CHABLIS

1½ cups CRACKER CRUMBS
1/3 cup melted BUTTER
1 pint OYSTERS, well drained
1/3 cup Calif. CHABLIS
½ cup CREAM or EVAPORATED MILK
1 cup grated CHEDDAR CHEESE

Mix crumbs and melted butter. Spread a layer over bottom of shallow baking dish (10x6x2). Cover with half the oysters and season. Repeat layers of crumbs, oysters and seasoning, topping with crumbs. Pour wine over all; add cream; sprinkle cheese on top. Bake at 425 F for 20 minutes. (Makes 3 servings)

BAKED HALIBUT

2 lb. HALIBUT or SEA BASS (1 thick slice)
1 small ONION, very thinly sliced
2 tablespoons BUTTER or MARGARINE
1 can (6 oz.) TOMATO PASTE
½ cup WATER
½ cup Calif. RED TABLE WINE
¼ cup finely chopped GREEN PEPPER
1 teaspoon SUGAR
SALT and PEPPER

Lay fish in a shallow baking dish. Add onion slices and dot with butter or margarine. Mix remaining ingredients, pour over fish. Bake (375 F) for 45 minutes, until fish flakes when tested with a fork. Baste fish with sauce during baking.

POACHED SOLE

1 cup WATER
½ cup California SAUTERNE
2 CHICKEN BOUILLON CUBES
1 small BAY LEAF
1 spring PARSLEY
¼ cup coarsely chopped GREEN ONION tops
¼ teaspoon PEPPERCORNS
4 FILETS OF SOLE (1 lb.)
8 small, fresh MUSHROOMS

Combine water, wine, chicken bouillon cubes, bay leaf, parsley, onion tops and peppercorns in a skillet. Heat to boiling. Fold fillets crosswise in half and place in skillet. Arrange mushrooms between fillets. Cover and simmer for 5 to 8 minutes, until fish is cooked through and flakes easily with a fork. Serve on warm platter with Wine Butter Sauce.

Wine Butter Sauce

2 tablespoons chopped GREEN ONION
½ cup BUTTER
¼ teaspoon CURRY POWDER
¼ cup Calif. SAUTERNE
2 tablespoons EACH:
Chopped PARSLEY
WINE VINEGAR

Cook chopped onion lightly in butter with curry powder for four minutes. Add Sauterne, plus parsley and wine vinegar. Heat gently and serve. (Makes 2/3 cup sauce)

SHERRY CUSTARD

¾ cup SUGAR
4 EGGS
¼ teaspoon SALT
1 teaspoon VANILLA
2 cups rich MILK
1/3 cup Calif. SHERRY

Melt 1/2 cup of sugar in heavy pan or skillet over moderate heat, stirring constantly til it forms a syrup. Pour into 5 or 6 buttered custard cups and set aside. Beat eggs lightly, then beat in remaining 1/4 cup sugar, salt, and vanilla. Stir in milk, then sherry. Pour into custard cups. Place cups in shallow pan; pour in about an inch of hot water to surround cups. Bake in a slow oven (325 F) for 40 minutes, or til custards are set in center. Remove cups from hot water, cool, then chill in refrigerator. Invert on serving dishes. (Makes 5 or 6 servings)

PEARS IN PORT WINE

4 fresh PEARS
1/3 cup SUGAR
½ cup Calif. PORT
1 tablespoon BUTTER

Cut pears in half and remove cores. Boil remaining ingredients. Pour over pears placed cut side down in greased baking dish. Bake 15 minutes at 350 F, basting frequently.

DUTCH APPLE CAKE

1 cup Calif. Cream SHERRY
4 whole CLOVES
4 whole ALLSPICE
3 medium size cooking APPLES
1¼ cups BISCUIT MIX
2 tablespoons SUGAR
3 tablespoons BUTTER or MARGARINE
MILK (about ¼ cup)
TOPPING

Heat sherry with spices in large skillet. Pare and core apples and cut in 8ths. Add apples to hot wine, cover, and cook 5 minutes. Uncover, turn apples, and cook, basting frequently, until tender. Remove apples with a slotted spoon. Turn wine into a measuring cup and cool.

Combine biscuit mix and sugar. Cut in butter til very fine. Add milk to reserved wine to measure 1/2 cup. Stir into the dry mixture to make a soft dough. Turn into a well-greased 8-inch layer cake pan, and arrange apple slices over top. Sprinkle with topping and bake in 375 F oven about 45 minutes, til cake tests done. Serve warm or cold. (Makes 6 servings)

Topping

2 tablespoons each: BISCUIT MIX, SUGAR
¼ teaspoon CINNAMON
1 tablespoon BUTTER

Combine all ingredients and blend until crumbly. Sprinkle over top of Dutch Apple Cake.

FRUIT COMPOTE

1 cup Calif. SWEET SAUTERNE
½ cup WATER
2 teaspoons finely chopped preserved GINGER
1 teaspoon SYRUP from ginger
4 whole ALLSPICE
1 strip LEMON PEEL, ½x2 inches
3 cups MELON BALLS
1 cup seedless GRAPES

Combine sauterne, water, ginger and syrup, allspice and lemon peel in a small saucepan. Bring to a boil, turn heat low and simmer, uncovered, 15 minutes. Strain syrup and cool. Combine with melon balls and grapes and chill.

STRAWBERRY PORT PIE

½ cup Calif. PORT
¾ cup WATER
1 (3-oz.) pkg. STRAWBERRY FLAVORED GELATIN
1 (12-oz.) pkg. frozen sliced STRAWBERRIES
2 teaspoons LEMON JUICE
1 (3-oz.) pkg. CREAM CHEESE
1 tablespoon MILK
1 (9-inch) baked PIE SHELL
WHIPPED CREAM

Heat wine and water to simmering; add gelatin and stir til dissolved. Remove from heat. Add frozen block of strawberries to the hot mixture. Let berries thaw, breaking up block with fork to speed process. Chill until mixture begins to thicken. Whip cream cheese and milk together with fork and spread evenly over bottom of pie shell. Pour in partially thickened gelatin mixture and chill til firm. Garnish with whipped cream.

ZABAGLIONE

5 EGG YOLKS
5 tablespoons SUGAR
5 tablespoons Calif. SHERRY
Pinch of SALT

Fill bottom of a double boiler with water and heat. Meanwhile, combine egg yolks, sugar and salt in top of double boiler and beat slightly. Beat sherry in very gradually. Set top of double boiler over heated water, and continue beating mixture til light (about 5 minutes) Serve in sherbet glasses or as sauce over pound cake. (Makes 4 servings)

QUICK 'N EASY WINE CAKE

1 pkg. Yellow CAKE MIX
1 pkg. Vanilla INSTANT PUDDING MIX
4 EGGS
¾ cup OIL
¾ cup Calif. SHERRY
1 teaspoon NUTMEG

Combine all ingredients. Mix with electric beater for 5 minutes at medium speed. Pour batter into greased angel food cake pan. Bake at 350 F about 45 minutes (or til done). Cool in pan for 5 minutes before turning out on rack. Sprinkle with powdered sugar.

Wine Drinks

SANGRIA

1 bottle (4/5 qt.) Calif. red table WINE
1 ORANGE
1 LEMON or 2 LIMES, sliced
3 tablespoons Calif. BRANDY
1 bottle (7 oz.) sparkling WATER
1 or 2 sliced fresh PEACHES
1 or 2 sliced PLUMS
½ cup fresh BERRIES
SUGAR to taste

Pour wine into glass pitcher. Peel orange in one long spiral strip. Put peel in wine, with one end of spiral curled over spout of pitcher. Squeeze orange; add juice to wine along with lemon and lime slices and brandy. Allow to stand several hours. One hour before serving, add remaining fruit. (Traditional Sangria is fruity, but not too sweet.) Before serving, add sparkling water. Pour Sangria into tall glasses half-filled with ice cubes. Add fruit to each glass. (Makes about 10 servings)

HOT BUTTERED WINE

1 can (6 oz.) frozen ORANGE JUICE CONCENTRATE
2 cups WATER
2 cups Calif. MUSCATEL
1/8 teaspoon CINNAMON
1/8 teaspoon NUTMEG
½ cup SUGAR
1 tablespoon BUTTER
½ fresh LEMON, sliced

Combine all ingredients in saucepan or chafing dish and stir til sugar dissolves. Heat steaming hot, but do not boil. Serve at once. (An electric slow-cooker pot, set on simmering, is excellent for hot wine drinks.)

SAUTERNE LEMONADE

1 can (6 oz.) frozen LEMONADE CONCENTRATE
2 cups cold WATER
1 bottle (4/5 qt.) Calif. SAUTERNE
ICE CUBES
MINT SPRIGS & LEMON SLICES

Empty can of lemonade concentrate into large pitcher. Add water, wine and ice cubes. Stir to blend. Add fresh lemon slices. Garnish with mint sprigs and other fruit in season. (Serves 8)

PARTY PUNCH

2 cups sliced fresh PEACHES
2 cups MELON BALLS
2 cups halved fresh STRAWBERRIES
¼ cup SUGAR
1 tablespoon LEMON JUICE
2 bottles (4/5 qt.) Calif. CHABLIS
2 bottles (4/5 qt.) Calif. CHAMPAGNE

Combine fruits, sugar, lemon juice and Chablis. Refrigerate several hours. Pour into chilled punch bowl over a small block of ice. Add chilled Champagne. (Makes 30 servings)

Brandy

BRANDIED PLUM PUDDING

1/3 cup BUTTER (soft)
¾ cup BROWN SUGAR (firmly packed)
1 EGG
2 tablespoons BRANDY
½ cup <u>each</u>: dried CURRANTS, chopped RAISINS, cut-up DATES
1/3 cup <u>each</u>: chopped CANDIED PINEAPPLE, CHERRIES, CITRON
1/3 cup PECANS
1 cup FLOUR
½ teaspoon SODA
¼ teaspoon <u>each</u>: SALT and CINNAMON
1/8 teaspoon <u>each</u>: ground ALLSPICE, GINGER, and NUTMEG
Granulated SUGAR

Cream together thoroughly, in a large mixing bowl, butter and brown sugar. Beat in egg and brandy. Stir in currants, raisins, dates, candied fruits, and pecans. Sift together into the fruit mixture the flour, soda, salt, and spices. Butter a five-cup mold well and sprinkle mold with sugar. Spoon mixture into mold and cover tightly. Place on a rack over boiling water in a covered kettle. Steam for four hours. Remove cover and turn out of mold while hot. Serve with brandy sauce.

(To serve flaming pudding, heat four tablespoons brandy in saucepan til just warm. Light brandy in saucepan and ladle flaming brandy over pudding.)

Brandy Hard Sauce

½ cup BUTTER (softened)
1½ cups sifted POWDERED SUGAR
3 tablespoons BRANDY

Beat butter til light and gradually beat in sifted sugar and brandy. Chill and serve with pudding.

CALIFORNIA EGGNOG

6 EGGS
6 tablespoons SUGAR
6 tablespoons WHISKEY
½ tablespoon grated NUTMEG
6 tablespoons BRANDY
3 tablespoons RUM
½ pint WHIPPING CREAM

Separate whites and yolks. Beat thoroughly (ESPECIALLY THE YOLKS). Add sugar to yolks and continue beating til smooth. Add whiskey and nutmeg and beat well. Fold in beaten whites. Add brandy and rum and beat thoroughly. Add cream (stiffly whipped), chill, and serve with dash of nutmeg.

LEMON-BRANDY PUNCH

2 LEMONS (Peel and Juice)
Pinch of CINNAMON
Dash of NUTMEG, MACE & CLOVES
¾ lb. SUGAR
½ pint boiling WATER
1 bottle Calif. BRANDY

Combine lemon peel and spices. Add sugar and boiling water. Let it simmer on the fire, then strain. Add brandy and juice of lemons. Set brandy afire before serving.

CHERRIES JUBILEE

1 can (1 lb.) BING CHERRIES
¼ cup BRANDY
1 tablespoon CORNSTARCH
1 tablespoon SUGAR
¼ cup pre-warmed BRANDY

Drain cherries thoroughly; put juice in saucepan. Pour brandy over cherries, and allow fruit to absorb brandy liquid for several hours. Before serving, moisten cornstarch and sugar with a little cold cherry juice. Add moistened cornstarch and sugar to cherry juice, cooking and stirring til thickened. Add brandied cherries and bring to boil. Pre-warm brandy. Pour heated cherries and syrup into flame-proof bowl and add pre-warmed brandy. Ignite mixture and spoon (use a heated spoon) flaming sauce over cherries. Serve over vanilla ice cream.

BRANDIED BALLS

1 (12-oz.) pkg. VANILLA WAFERS (crushed fine)
¼ cup BRANDY
¼ cup RUM
¼ to ½ cup HONEY
1 lb. WALNUTS (ground fine)

Mix all ingredients together well. Roll into small balls. Then roll in powdered sugar. Store in tightly-covered container in refrigerator. (Will keep for one month)

BRANDY PUNCH

½ cup SUGAR
¾ cup WATER
6 strips LEMON PEEL
12 CLOVES
3-inch STICK CINNAMON
1 cup ORANGE JUICE
½ cup LEMON JUICE
1 cup JUICE of CANNED PEARS
1 pint Calif. BRANDY
1½ cup SPARKLING WATER

Boil together sugar, water, lemon peel, cloves, and cinnamon for five minutes. Cool and strain. Add remainder of ingredients. Pour over ice block in punch bowl and garnish with fruit.

TROPICAL AMBROSIA

6 whole peeled ORANGES
CONFECTIONERS SUGAR
3 ripe BANANAS
2 cups freshly-grated COCONUT
2 tablespoons APRICOT BRANDY

Place oranges (round side down) on cutting board and cut crosswise in thin slices. Cover bottom of a glass bowl with a layer of orange slices. Sprinkle with sugar, add a layer of bananas and one of grated coconut. Repeat layers. Before adding final topping of grated coconut, sprinkle brandy over fruit. Top with coconut and chill. (Makes six servings)

CAFE ROYALE

Add brandy to coffee and sweeten to taste. Twist small strip of lemon peel into cup and serve.

Index

A

B

C

D

E

F

G

H

I

J

K

L

M

N

O

P

Q

R

S

T

V

Z

Notes

ORDER BLANK

Send a taste of California to a friend! CALIFORNIA 5-in-1 COOKBOOK mailed anywhere for $3 (plus 50¢ postage and handling).

Name ______________________________

Address ______________________________

City ____________________ State _____ Zip _____

Name ______________________________

Address ______________________________

City ____________________ State _____ Zip _____

Name ______________________________

Address ______________________________

City ____________________ State _____ Zip _____

Please mail _____ copies of CALIFORNIA 5-in-1 COOKBOOK to the above. I enclose $__________.

My name ______________________________

Address ______________________________

City ____________________ State _____ Zip _____